Westhope

Westhope

LIFE AS A FORMER FARM BOY

Dean Hulse

University of Minnesota Press

Minneapolis

London

Published by the University of Minnesota Press
111 Third Avenue South, Suite 290
Minneapolis, MN 55401-2520
http://www.upress.umn.edu

Library of Congress Cataloging-in-Publication Data

Hulse, Dean.
    Westhope : life as a former farm boy / Dean Hulse.
        p. cm.
    ISBN 978-0-8166-6512-9 (hbk. : acid-free paper)
    1. Hulse, Dean. 2. Hulse, Dean—Childhood and youth.
3. Hulse, Dean—Family. 4. Westhope (N.D.)—Biography.
5. Westhope (N.D.)—Social life and customs. 6. Farm life—
North Dakota—Westhope. I. Title.
    F644.W47H85 2009
    978.4´61—dc22
    [B]
                                    2008053980

Printed in the United States of America on acid-free paper

The University of Minnesota is an equal-opportunity educator and employer.

15 14 13 12 11 10 09   10 9 8 7 6 5 4 3 2 1

Passing, in due course, the now familiar camping places of Wood End, the Souris River crossings, Turtle Mountain, etc., it was not without regret that they were left behind for the last time; and, despite the many disadvantages of the prairie and plains, there is no doubt that persons who have spent much time on them, acquire a sort of attachment to them that more pleasing landscapes fail to inspire. What the reason of this may be it is difficult to say; but the feeling is probably the same as that which a sailor has for the sea.

—Capt. Albany Featherstonhaugh, R.E.,
Narrative of the Operations of the British North American Boundary Commission (1872–76)

And all the while I was alone,
the past was close behind

—Bob Dylan, "Tangled Up in Blue" (1974)

Contents

Introduction

I am a lifelong North Dakota resident, a farm boy, and yet I've spent fewer than half my years living on a farm. Our home sits in the midsection of North Dakota's largest city. Although Fargo is not my hometown, it has served as a vantage point for my conflicts. I fled small-town life when Jimmy Carter was president. Burning within me at the time was a desire to be as unlike rural people as possible—especially unlike my parents. However, even with the passing of time, the imprints of small-town culture remain clearly tattooed on my consciousness.

Meanwhile, memories about the joys and sorrows of my adolescent and early adult years have been evolving. Anger I once directed mercilessly at my parents gave way to an understanding that became more complex with their deaths. This transformative comprehension has grown from the rootstock of appreciation, forgiveness, and gratefulness—which is to say, love. I have become an ironical prodigal.

In many ways, and not surprisingly, I am a composite of my parents' personalities, mirror images included: solitary yet friendly, emotionally stingy yet materially generous, hard-hearted yet sentimental, happy yet melancholy. Where I differ from my parents has been in self-perception. My parents lived a more cloistered life with close-knit relationships and flourished in those roles. I sought a broader stage without a spotlight, providing anonymity. I got what I wanted, but I now believe independence becomes a weak sister when she is standing next to a type of interdependence made possible through shared experience, mutual respect, and trust.

These days I mimic many of my parents' and grandparents' behaviors. Two particular hand-me-downs are a respect for the land and a disdain for social and economic injustices. Because of my inheritances, I have become consumed by causes related to protecting the land and preserving rural communities. At the same time, I hold a less sentimental view than my ancestors in that I see the prairie landscape and country people through a split screen—that is, as beautiful and as helpful as one could hope, as harsh and as cold as one might dare imagine.

No doubt, I am living an in-between life, unlike the thousands of farm boys and farm girls who have left the state never to return and unlike many of my friends who never left the farm or my hometown. Consequently, my experiences are neither worldly nor small-town static. I've driven by Paris, Illinois, never been to its French namesake. I understand the viewpoint of those who feel diminished by their rural upbringing, but I also appreciate what farming and small-town living can teach.

According to Songfacts, a searchable database, Bob Dylan wrote "Tangled Up in Blue" while residing on a Minnesota farm he had just bought. The song reflects personal changes Dylan was experiencing at the time, and he has frequently introduced the piece to live audiences by saying it took "ten years to live and two years to write."

Growing up near the Canadian border and having lived on a farm are the only experiences I dare claim to share with the prolific Mr. Dylan. But as with "Tangled Up in Blue," the highly personal essays I offer in this collection took more years to live than write. Some are "cultural studies" of a time that is my yesterday. Others are rants—not about change per se, but about the status quo or bald-faced boosterism packaged as change that is "inevitable" or evidence of "progress." Are super-duper mega marts and Wall Street equitable proxies for mom-and-pop shops and Main Street? I don't think so. Unaccountable corporative growth is not a substitute for development resulting from small-scale entrepreneurship but rather it is dystopia masquerading as a marketplace marvel, a construct of unchecked optimism and intellectual sloth.

Of course, people can and often do disagree. I understand we all lead unique lives and have developed individualized perspectives, but when writing these essays I labored under the belief that we might reach similar conclusions about experiences involving personal growth and affronts to our sense of place and community. An only child, I often have been cut by aloneness— of facing, without the benefit of siblings, life's sharpest-edged realities, such as the illness and loss of parents. At times, my knowledge and experiences comfort. At other times, I question whether I fit in anywhere.

I know more than most city folks about agriculture, but a lot less than any good farmer or rancher. I've studied the teachings of visionaries such as Wes Jackson, founder of the Land Institute and promoter of perennial polycultures—that is, various crops growing symbiotically in the same field. Among the benefits of this concept is the need to replant only after a span of many years and, thereby, reduced production costs for farmers. Likewise, Allan

Savory's Holistic Management has opened my eyes to the possibilities of using history to craft a future—that is, using the past as the vehicle for forward momentum. Savory's idea of planned recovery grazing involves using beef cattle and other domesticated livestock to mimic the instinctive habits of the bison herds that once roamed the Great Plains. Sustainable ideas, both.

For the land and its people: a phrase often used to describe the mission of the U.S. land grant system. However, after working in the ag college of a land grant university, I'm left to wonder whether researchers and administrators there care at all about reducing a farmer's production costs. As a result of Jackson, Savory, and others—Wendell Berry, first and foremost—I've reached conclusions about what's been occurring in rural America during my life that diverge from general opinion.

I strive to be hopeful. America still is a democracy. People can vote and alter any policy. Furthermore, they can influence whether or how the U.S. Constitution is amended. But I often am not optimistic. Frequently, I'm mad as hell because I perceive the loss of something beautiful and needful: agriculture in the fullest sense of the word—that is, acres and culture. Those who are kind, or at least tolerant, intending their diction to carry a positive connotation, call me an activist, a trait I acquired from Dad perhaps by way of genetics as well as modeled behavior.

Of course, my story is unfinished because I still haven't been able to press all that which is crumpling my insides. Weekly, it seems, I've reflected on my younger days growing up on a farm (and farming for a while) and being part of a community of country folk. Dad's influence, largely. The prairie landscape and people. A love for and familiarity with the land so keen that I still can recall where rocks lie waiting to be plucked after a spring's thaw has pushed the irregular orbs to the surface. Where sloughs sit and perennially scheme to bog down a tractor. The shady cottonwoods where Dad and I enjoyed afternoon lunches with neighbors during haying season.

Those lunches, for example, featuring peanut butter laid thick on homemade brown bread, along with honey or chokecherry jelly. Lunches completed with rhubarb pie or maybe moist, cakey oatmeal-raisin cookies. Authentic homemade food, plus all the traditions of growing, preparing, and sharing meals with family and friends. Mom's influence, mostly.

The prairie landscape and its abundance, yes, but people, too. A familiarity with people, most now dead, so keen that I could identify their approach by the rhythm of their footsteps, could foresee the motion of the hand they would use as a greeting when our cars passed, could predict when their character flaws might surface or what actions or words might prompt that exposure.

I miss the land and the people who live close to it. I need both. There's a part of me that fills with peacefulness only when I'm in the country, of that much I'm absolutely certain. But how do acres and culture become agriculture for me? Answering that question represents a leg of my life's journey, one necessarily more urgent now that more of my time on this earth resides in the bottom of the hourglass than in its top. Weeks now seem to go by faster than the days when I was in grade school waiting for the afternoon bell to ring.

What to do? For me, standing pat isn't an option. I want to draw from a deck of revitalizing possibilities.

Gazing into the future, I'm beginning to discern the inchoate outline for a new life—a rebirth, really—that might very well be worth the trouble of transplanting myself in the countryside, next to people who, if experience is any guide, might become familiar, frequent pains in the ass with whom I could learn to feel right at home.

Main Street

My freshest memories took form in the aftermath of thunderstorms and were baptized in rain-washed breezes. My imprint includes the sinking sun as it favors Turtle Mountain with a brilliant spotlight, and farther east, a bank of blue-black clouds is a scrim. The musical score accompanying this production rides on the meadowlarks' melody, a sound as refreshing to the ear as cold water is to the throat, a sound as resonant as that resulting from the delicate fingernail-thump of fine crystal.

And so it was on many Saturday evenings, as Dad, Mom, and I eased along the two-and-a-half-mile stretch of U.S. Highway 83 that took us into Westhope, North Dakota, my hometown. Our greeter was the public swimming pool, sitting in the northeast corner of town along the highway, the outskirts then. The pool often overflowed with kids—mostly town kids, as active as ants before a rain. Immediately to the south of the pool was the drive-in, its man-size plastic ice-cream cone beckoning, promising a luxurious end to an evening filled with friendly adult conversation and youthful exploration.

Unlike Mom's maternal grandparents and her parents, my folks no longer made this weekly trip out of a need to barter butter and eggs for salt, flour, and other staples. Nor did we even need to stock up on necessities or other

1

store-bought items. Instead, we made our jaunts to town for the purpose of spending a new commodity: leisure time, made possible by postwar prosperity, the swapping of horseflesh for horsepower, and various other horse trades I later came to understand.

When we arrived, Dad slipped into a preferred parking slot along the two-block wall of buildings that hugged both sides of Main Street's business district. As Dad's right hand was turning off the ignition, mine was reaching for the door handle.

My adventures each week were funded by a quarter that had been warming in my pocket since after supper, and my first stop was the Rexall drugstore, which had two counters full of penny candy and another of the nickel-and-dime variety. Occasionally, I partook of a chocolate-flavored Coke with some toasted cashews tossed in, a concoction that set me back fifteen cents. The druggist had a two-tiered nut display, with heat lights, right next to the soda fountain. The top tier was filled with trays of exotic nuts such as white and red pistachios. The bottom tier was a large round rotating container, its assortment enhanced by light dancing on the oily nutmeats.

From the drugstore I sauntered to the hardware store, two buildings to the south, where my plans called for no cash outlays. Instead, my visits were merely to keep tabs on the inventory—to make sure no new bicycles or baseball gloves had come in since my last tour—and to watch enviously one of the few color TVs in town. Another routine: stepping on a loose board in the middle aisle (of the three aisles) to get the glass covers on the cookware rattling.

Directly across the street from the hardware store was something more intriguing than merchandise: rusting metal with jagged edges. Irresistible. I was lured to the old conveyor in the same way a fish is attracted to a daredevil hook. The conveyor must have been designed for moving gravel or some such heavy material, coal probably, and it sat about fifty feet from the Main Street sidewalk along a narrow gap between buildings. Mounting that conveyor and then tiptoeing along it east to the alley brought a special challenge on Saturday nights because torn dress pants could inform Mom that I'd walked through the forbidden zone, an alcove created by the space where one building ended and another began. A volunteer ash tree gave this makeshift town square for kids a domesticated feel, and next to the tree is where hoodlums huddled to smoke their cigarettes.

The conveyor led adventurers to an alley and a rusting metal container nearly as large as the box on a grain truck, which served as the trash bin for one of the town's bars, the Can-Dak. Streetlight reflections flickered and sometimes hid among the beveled designs of discarded liquor bottles and allowed my sense of vision to override my sense of smell and the essence of a sweetly rotten swill. When the boozy stench became overpowering, I took the alley north a block, swung west a block, and cut next to the community hall, built before my time in 1939 by President Franklin Roosevelt's Works Progress Administration (or "WPA," as Mom and Dad called it).

Behind the community hall, beyond another alley, sat the hotel, owned by Howard Henry, a farmer-politician who almost single-handedly got parking meters removed from the state. Many of the townsfolk, including me, swelled with pride when conversations with strangers turned to the subject of hometowns. Upon hearing the name of my hometown, they might ask, "Isn't that where Howard Henry's from?"

The Gateway Hotel was a small-town amalgamation: hotel, restaurant, bar, basement apartments, movie theater, jewelry store, and beauty parlor. I often cut downstairs through the apartment hallway and then came up and out another exit that was next to the entrance for the theater. Movies didn't interest me much in the summertime, when the sun didn't set until well past nine o'clock (in the era before daylight saving time). My last few cents usually went for an assortment from the candy case in the hotel lobby.

Not every Saturday night went this way. Sometimes I hooked up with a friend or two, but I wasn't eager to keep friendships going when I had a whole quarter to spend, so I usually kept to myself. Sometimes I sat in the lilac bush near the graveled parking lot on the hotel's north side. That bush was, in fact, two bushes that had grown together. A person could crawl in and be sitting inside these lilac bushes looking out, and people on the outside were clueless as to the presence hiding within, unless they'd spent some time inside the bushes themselves.

I had discovered the lilac bushes' secret when I was playing hide-and-seek during vacation Bible school at the Masonic Temple nearby. For a time it seemed that I was the only Presbyterian my age who knew about the hideaway. I wondered whether any city kids were wise to the lilac bushes. I doubted that any farm kids who were Catholics or Lutherans knew because their churches were on the other side of town. Eventually, I decided to share my knowledge with Kevin and Keith Martin, fellow Presbyterians and biological twins as different as siblings can be. One of them blabbed away the spot's uniqueness to Steve Seiffert, also a Presbyterian who lived close enough to town to be part of the city crowd. Soon, the bushes became another hideaway where juveniles could smoke (and occasionally share with me) their Salems and Winstons and Old Golds.

In addition to Saturday night get-togethers, Main Street hosted celebrations such as the Fourth of July, when the city fathers sometimes hired a carnival and the southernmost block filled with rides, side shows, concessions, carnies, and, eventually, revelers. One time I was about to get on the Ferris wheel for a solo ride when a greaser (cigarette pack rolled in a shirt sleeve) jumped in line beside me. The Ferris wheel operator paired us up. My "partner" was a stranger to me and drunk besides. Mom was intolerant of drinkers, and so I suppose she was partly responsible for my fear and loathing of this man, whose breath wafted on the night air and reminded me of the garbage can behind the Can-Dak.

Once we got to the very top of the Ferris wheel, the operator stopped the ride to let some more people on. Probably in his twenties (which seemed to me then an age where one is old enough to know better), my drunk companion began rocking our seat—violently. The only thing that kept me from becoming a splat on Main Street that night was the seat's safety bar, a one-inch-square piece of wood extending across the seat, secured by a flimsy latch that decided, for some reason, not to let go, thank God. I don't think I ever rode on a Ferris wheel again.

Besides professional entertainment, we usually had some homegrown fun on the Fourth, too. One year, a group of businessmen lined up on one side of Main Street and a group of farmers formed a team on the other. These gladiators battled each other with two fire hoses spewing high-pressure blasts of water. Another year, some adults thought the kids might enjoy looking for a needle in a haystack, literally, and so some farmer contributed a pile of loose straw, within which ten sewing needles allegedly hid. I can't recall whether anyone found a needle. I didn't, but then, I wasn't really trying.

There was dancing in the Community Hall to end these festivities: polkas, schottisches, and such that people my parents' age liked. While the adults were dancing, the group I hung with explored some of the neighborhoods a few blocks away from Main Street. It was too early, most years, for the crab apples to be big enough to throw at cars, so we figured out other ways to make older kids and strangers of various ages angry enough to chase us.

Name-calling usually worked. Creative stuff. A driver's last name rhymed with slurs that became more risqué with age. Never anything as pedestrian as "Hey, numb nuts." Few of us ever got caught. I never did, even though I was fat and slow. There's really nothing like the exhilaration of being scared witless enough to hurdle thigh-high picket fences in dress pants. Or to be hiding beneath a pickup truck while the person who is imagining that his hands are squeezing your throat is standing only an arm's length away.

Of course, some thrill-seeking stunts were just plain stupid, such as the time I tried stealing food from one of the grocery stores. I chose cheese because of where the cooler sat, in an aisle out of sight from the cashier's counter. As I was about to slip the Cracker Barrel into my inside jacket pocket, I sensed the heat of someone's eyes, which turned out to be those of the storekeeper, Terry Baumann. He just shook his head, and I promptly put the cheese back. It was months before I dared go back in the store and face him.

Just north of that grocery store, across a graveled parking lot, stood the town's only Laundromat, a not-so-clean, well-lighted place in which a high-energy bluish glow ricocheted off rows of white enamel. The Laundromat was mostly a hangout for kids, such as Tommy Kleespie, who went there to smoke. Older than I (and hopefully odder too), Tommy ate bugs for a dime. For anyone producing a dollar, he drank fresh pig's blood at the butcher shop across the street from his home. One evening when I was "killing time" at the Laundromat, waiting for Mom and Dad's Farmers Union meeting at the Odd Fellows Hall to end, Tommy explained to me the art, and seeming necessity, of masturbation. For free.

North of the Laundromat stood Clark's Repair, run by Clark Palmer, not one for mincing words. Keith Berentson, the youngest of many hell-raiser brothers with soft hearts, mostly, once brought the car he'd inherited from his grandpa to Clark for some work. Keith's first car, it was a bronze-colored '63 Chevy four-door sedan. As Keith delighted in telling his story, Clark listened to the motor idle for several minutes and then said, "Could be any of a thousand things wrong with this cocksucker." After Clark had worked his magic, Keith came back to pick up his car and, with equal delight, recalled many times Clark's sage advice: "Keith, you've got a nice little car here. But if you keep roddin' it the way you've been doin', it ain't goin' to last. It just ain't goin' to last."

The Chevy didn't last. And neither did a succession

of Keith's cars, one of which he rolled—not side to side but end over end—in Antler, North Dakota. Nor finally did Keith, who died in another car crash years later.

Next door to Clark's Repair was a bar, the second floor of which was home to the local VFW chapter. Every fall, the veterans put on a hamburger feed for all the boys who'd played Little League baseball the previous summer. Each year for not enough years, the smells of hot grease and onions frying on the grill greeted us Little Leaguers, followed by all the hamburgers and soda pop we could eat or drink topped off with a free pass to the Saturday night movie and buttered popcorn.

Of course times and people change, and so did Main Street. I moved through grade school and into high school, and we did what high schoolers in the area had been doing for years: we drove to a neighboring town for the Saturday night dances. Meanwhile, the older farm folks eventually stopped coming to town on Saturday nights. The trend that had begun during my parents' life only amplified itself—that is, the horsepower of machines replaced not only horses but humans as well, and so, there were larger farms and fewer farmers. And those who remained in the countryside didn't feel the need to visit one another as much, even though cars made visiting easier than in the horse-and-buggy or horse-and-sleigh days.

Mom and Dad began making their trips to town on Saturday night later in the evening because of television and Saturday night icons such as Jackie Gleason and North Dakota native Lawrence Welk. Also, Sunday night visits at neighbors' homes became less frequent, what with *The Wonderful World of Disney* and *Bonanza* streaming into our living rooms.

And once everyone got color TVs, cozy home entertainment seemed the most logical option on cold winter nights, or anytime, really, except of course on holidays, birthdays, and high school graduations. For a natural-born visitor like Dad, the telephone became an essential accessory. Meanwhile, we enjoyed laughing at ourselves through such interrelated living-color sitcoms as *The Beverly Hillbillies,* featuring a greedy banker, a villain figure for almost any farmer; *Petticoat Junction,* with a bevy of beautiful country girls; and *Green Acres,* with a big-city lawyer whose irrational move to the countryside transformed him into one of the more rational members of his farming community.

When I was a freshman in high school, Westhope underwent a foreshadowing physical change. The hardware store, a café, the drugstore, and a vacant building that had housed a dry cleaners burned to the ground. The hardware owner confidently rebuilt, but the owner of the café never did. The pharmacist relocated down the street and patiently planned the construction of his new building (half the size of the hardware store but with a new soda fountain). Later on, the post office moved to the brick building next to the temporary drug store, and the old post office became a ceramics shop, a bakery, and then I think it burned down, too.

During some of that transition, I went to college, got married, and came home to farm in 1978. It took only two growing seasons for Nicki and me to conclude, too quickly, that some aspects of small-town living were not what Norman Rockwell had pictured: nosiness passing for concern, for example, and some father–son partnerships—Dad's and mine, for instance.

We moved to Fargo in 1979, and eventually a lot of other people living in and around Westhope departed, too. Those who stayed, persisted. A group of community-minded investors formed a city-owned corporation when the Gateway Hotel burned down; they built a new hotel-restaurant-bar complex (minus a movie theater) costing hundreds of thousands of dollars—the Gateway Inn. And then the town got a new employer, a mail-order clothing business housed where the town's last farm equipment dealership had been.

In the mid-1990s, we attended a family reunion in the old community hall (demolished in 2001). A group of us were standing outside drinking beers when two old-timers came shuffling up. Shy Ragnar Warner, still perfecting his silent treatment, and Collin ("Collie") Seiffert lived catty-corner northeast from the hall in apartments built where the ice-skating rink used to be. Collie asked us what was going on.

"It's a family reunion," a couple of us said.

"Farmers Union?"

"No. Family reunion," some of us yelled. When it became obvious Collie still hadn't gotten it, Nicki tried another tactic. She said, "Your son, Stevie, went to school with Dean," and then she pointed to me.

"Crosby? I've got a daughter who teaches in Crosby."

We gave up on conversation and listened instead to a well-rehearsed monologue. Collie told us that he was ninety-two (he lived to be ninety-eight) and that Ragnar was nearing ninety. Then shaking his head, Collie said, "No. There's not much future for guys like us." With that, he and Ragnar, both clad in sweaters on a Sunday afternoon in July, ambled home for what I'm sure was to be several hours of napping.

When Nicki and I moved home to farm, there wasn't a house to rent in town. Now, elderly widows occupy many of the houses. One of the last times Nicki and I were in Westhope on the Fourth of July, we watched a parade, which, along with an occasional demolition derby, has replaced the carnival as a means of celebration. The Fourth of July parade we saw wasn't much. The town's new secondhand fire truck served as one of the floats. Another float was a convertible filled (except for the driver) with white- and blue-haired women, all members of the local garden club. The float following the convertible was nothing more than a lawn tractor pulling a little utility wagon. A hand-stenciled sign in the wagon read "WESTHOPE ARTS COUNCIL."

Nicki said, "I think that sign's missing an F."

Sometimes I don't know whether to laugh or cry. When Mom and Dad retired, they built a new home in town just behind the drive-in, directly southeast and across a drainage ditch from the swimming pool. They built because there weren't any existing houses for sale at the time. Dad died in 1992, and in 2003, I was staying at Mom's house during her brief hospitalization in Minot before she died. On one of those nights I was awakened by the volunteer firefighters, trying in vain to save the drive-in.

In recent years, the owner of the floral shop built a new showroom and greenhouse. The floral shop had occupied the former drugstore. Before that, the floral shop was located in a former appliance store and subsequent dry cleaners, which has since become the Heartland Café. The lone grocery store has reopened and continues providing a valuable service to Westhope residents because otherwise the nearest grocery store is thirty miles away. The Gateway Inn became the Elkhorn Lodge, which experienced a fire in its restaurant and eventually reopened as the community-owned Gateway Motel, with the restaurant space housing city offices and a library. The pluck of these people astounds me.

One of the last times I was home before Mom died, it was hot: the first weekend of August, which usually coincided with her birthday on the fourth. After supper and cake, Nicki and I decided to go for a walk, and we ended up on Main Street. There were cars parked in front of the senior citizens' center, a former clothing store, for Saturday night bingo. Over one block to the north, a car sat in the spot where Uncle Chet, Dad's brother, and Aunt Evelyn always parked on those Saturday nights so many years before (when, with prompting from Evelyn, Chet dispensed nickels, dimes, or more, to a favorite nephew). Chet and Evelyn's spot was on the east side of the Jack and Jill grocery store, which Terry Baumann, the last of the Baumann grocers going back more than ninety years, sold when he retired. A few more cars sat in front of the Can-Dak bar.

If the current drinking scene is the same as it was when I lived and drank in Westhope, then locals recognize many of the cars parked near this liquor establishment as belonging to alcohol abusers and alcoholics, both as persistent as Canada thistle. As we were walking along in the August heat that night, I began thinking about the people I had known growing up. Westhope has produced lawyers, doctors, nurses, pharmacists, veterinarians, accountants, workaday cowboys, professional athletes, ministers, priests, social workers, journalists, teachers, farmers, musicians, artists, laborers, clerks, chefs, heroes who served in the armed forces and died, and felons who served in prison and lived to tell about it.

At one point on our walk that night, Nicki and I encountered Edith Huber heading home from visiting a friend, or perhaps she had been making a late trip to the post office. As a younger woman, Edith possessed lustrous black hair that complemented her broadly set eyes and high cheekbones. For years Edith worked for Howard Henry at the Gateway Hotel, and on many youthful Saturday nights I spent my last dime on candy beckoning to me from beneath a glass display case. Edith fetched that candy with slender hands accented by well-manicured bright red nails.

When we met, Edith asked, "Isn't it hot?"

"Yes," we said. "It sure is."

And that was it: end of conversation. Edith, her gray hair still set in a practical combed-back style, wore a light dress that reminded me of a housecoat (perhaps it was). She continued on her way, and we moved in the opposite direction. After a moment, I turned back toward Edith. She had become a silhouette.

The Barn

T he sound came from somewhere out of the east. A
rhythmic chanting. "Dad, Dad, listen. Indians."

I smelled hay and manure. In the background
I heard the muffled contentment of horses chomping
oats. The setting sun had gilded granaries, fields, shelterbelts—everything. No wind, a temperature still comforting enough to ensure no threat of snow, no foreboding,
only the gauzy stillness of an autumn sunset.

Dad had just finished chores. I was standing outside
our barn when I heard the singing. Since I was only four
or five at the time, my conclusion relied on limited experience, much of which had come from watching television
and the so-called cowboy-and-Indian shows of the 1950s,
as well as from my understanding that the Turtle Mountain Indian Reservation was situated at some distance to
the east of our farm. I thought I was listening to a pow-
wow, and I was scared.

Dad chuckled gently: not Indians, but snow geese.
Years later I understood how in that moment, our barn
became my cocoon.

I spent a lot of time in our barn with Dad, so much, in
fact, that he felt obliged to make me a time-occupying
swing fashioned from a loop of heavy rope tied in two
places to a support beam. At the base of the loop Dad had
wedged a wooden seat he'd whittled. I suspect the idea

for a swing came to Dad after my encounter with Dolly, a large pinto mare. Dad once looked up from his milking stool to see where I was and, to his horror, saw me stroking Dolly's tail. I was positioned perfectly for a swift kick in the head.

Dad helped build our barn, which has a rounded roof, unlike neighboring gambrel or lean-to designs. Images and sensations I associate with the barn occupy many of my thoughts still: the oily leather of the harnesses, halters, bridles, and saddles; horse sweat, permeating saddle blankets, the entire barn; feed troughs, worn smooth not by sandpaper and human hand but by bovine or equine tongues licking up the last of the "chop," Dad's custom-ground oats.

As soon as I was strong and coordinated enough to wield a pitchfork, Dad taught me how to stack manure, a necessary skill for keeping a barn clean. Manure and urine and straw form a sulfurous building material that is functional in the same way bricks or blocks are. To build a load of manure, we slid the tines of our pitchforks into the tripartite slickness, lifted, balanced, and placed the acrid squares onto each corner of the stoneboat (a four-by-eight-foot piece of heavy wood mounted on skids). Then, the forkfuls went along the stoneboat's sides, and finally, its front and back. We built this outer wall about three feet tall before we heaped the center with looser, sloppier matter, most of which came from the gutters behind the stalls. We scooped the slop with a rusty grain shovel, and this job taught me a quick-flicking wrist action I still use for many tasks, such as moving slushy snow or picking up sawdust piles.

As I grew older, Saturdays were when we cleaned the barn most thoroughly because I was not in school and time was not a consideration. Depending upon which horses were living or dead, Dad harnessed Dolly and Patches, or Dolly and Candy, or Candy and Bonnie and then hooked the team to our stoneboat. We stacked and talked while the horses' hot breath fogged small portions of the barn. When we became silent, I listened to the swish-swishing of tails accompanying the fluttery sound of steamy air escaping through flappy horse lips. After building a load, Dad told the team to "come up," and the sturdy sculpture slid along for about a quarter mile out to the manure pile in the horse pasture. We repeated this process for as long and as many loads as it took to make the barn animal-waste free.

As Dad hauled the last load out to the manure pile, I scattered fresh straw over the cleaned surfaces. I retrieved the straw from our haymow, which we entered by climbing a flight of stairs connected to the barn's northwest wall. I sent the bales I selected in our haymow hurtling down the stairway, crashing onto the floor below. The impact of plant residue on concrete produced dust, which floated on the barn's angled sunlight and exposed the subterfuge of spiders. Before an elementary teacher introduced me to Charlotte and long before E. B. White was teaching me how to write with style, I was mesmerized by the intricacy of the arachnids' artistry.

The last step in our barn-cleaning ritual always came in two parts: first, coaxing the animals back into their respective stalls and pens; and second, watching with some degree of dismay, because within minutes streams or steaming piles marked the start of another cycle.

Along with the relentless recycling of animal waste, I witnessed many births in our barn. Often on frosty

late-winter mornings we came into our barn, warm and
humid from animal bodies and breath, to find a newborn
calf standing next to its mother. At other times, when a
calf's legs and head were out of alignment with nature's
order, I observed as Dad and a neighbor extracted it using
our calf puller. Old-fashioned compared to current designs, our calf puller was composed of a pulley, enough
rope for attaching to a nearby support beam and for grab-
bing to produce hand-over-hand leverage, and chain, for
wrapping around a calf's front legs. The experience of
Dad and his neighbors, and their skill with the calf puller,
could overcome nearly every type of birthing problem. If
not, we called the vet and hoped that education succeeded
where experience and brawn had failed.

For smaller animals, such as our sheep (purebred
Suffolk), the force needed to aid birth was less demanding. One time when I was eight or nine and Dad had gone
to an all-day political meeting, Mom and I aided a struggling ewe. Expecting problems, Dad had penned the ewe
in the barn and warned us that she might have trouble.
Mom and I kept a vigilant watch by checking her every
hour. By late morning, the ewe's water had broken, but
she remained standing. Mom noticed only one hoof protruding and told me to position the wooden gate so that
it restricted the ewe's movement to a triangular corner of
the pen. Then Mom rolled up a shirtsleeve, washed her
right arm up to her elbow with a diluted solution of Lysol
and warm water, and began sliding her hand, then her
arm, into the ewe's birth canal. She kept her forearm inside the slippery darkness, probing with her fingers, until
she found the wandering hoof. With hoof in hand, Mom
began removing her arm slowly from the ewe, guiding the

hoof toward daylight. Once Mom's arm was free, she coaxed the ewe to lie down. The ewe began pushing, and Mom began pulling on the lamb's front legs. At one point, Mom shook a hand violently, and a piece of afterbirth about the size of a pencil eraser flew from her fingertips and landed on my upper lip. Because I needed both hands to keep the gate in place, I stood there, gagging, eyes tearing, unable to come to my own aid, until Mom laid a steaming lamb onto a carpet of fresh straw.

Other births occurred in our barn, too. When our farm cats (mousers, not pets) decided to have kittens, they usually chose one of two places, both of which offered a soft bed: the haymow or a feed bunk. Many times while feeding our horses, I discovered a mother with kittens nestled on a cushion of hay. The horses, their heads buried in the feed bunk, large, rubbery lips grasping at stems of hay, were gracious hosts.

Of course, not all our calves, lambs, or kittens survived. Death moves among all livestock herds with regularity, a fact farmers and ranchers reluctantly accept: "If you're going to raise livestock, you're going to have some dead stock." And so, a few deaths linger in my memory.

I remember Tony, the Welsh pony, a gift from Grandpa and Grandma Trimble to my cousin "Kip," who once had fallen out of Grandpa and Grandma's moving car. Mom said this accident had produced a guilt that affected my grandparents' decisions concerning Kip. Tony also was the equine embodiment of a verbal agreement between Grandpa and Grandma and Kip, who promised never to smoke in exchange for getting the pony.

Because Kip's family lived at the time in Westhope, we kept Tony on our farm, just a few miles north of town.

My memories are so melded that it seems as though we had visitors every night during the summers when Tony was alive, but of course that can't be true. When I think of Tony, I see Kip's friends, boys nearly a decade older than I who, along with Kip, spoiled Tony by running full speed at Tony's rump, placing their hands on his hips, and using their momentum to lift themselves over his haunches and into the saddle. Tony reacted to this unwelcome treatment by becoming hard to handle. The best example of his stubbornness was his bucking, a trick he resorted to whenever and wherever he tired of carrying riders.

One hot summer day in July, Mom and I pulled into our farmyard and were shocked to see maroonish black streaks all along the west side of our barn, and on one side of the white-board fence making up our corral. Only in the horse trough did the blood maintain its color of just-spilled redness. Tony had had a nosebleed.

After consulting the vet, Dad and Uncle Cliff, Kip's dad, gave Tony a shot, but months later we found him dead in the pasture. He was lying in a dried patch of his own blood. The day the animal-disposal truck pulled out of our pasture, Dad and I stood alone on our driveway and watched the truck fade into the landscape. Cliff accepted Tony's death like a farmer, with resignation. Kip's silence spoke for his loss.

Along with Tony the pony's death, there were the deaths, spread across many years, of many farm dogs. Spike, a border collie, had been with Mom and Dad before I was born. He loved to herd cattle. Dad need only say, "Sic 'em, Spike," and he would duck under the barbed wire fence and be on a dead run for the pasture. Mom's photo albums contain pictures of me as a chubby toddler trying to ride Spike like a horse. There are other snapshots of Spike walking alongside a team of horses, and of Spike standing next to Tony the pony.

As he got older and acquired the hip pain of old age, Spike would lie with his rear legs pointed away from his body rather than tucked underneath him. As dogs are wont to do, Spike liked to lie in the shade of large objects on hot summer days, and once during haying season a hasty neighbor neglected to look for Spike before pulling a full load of hay toward the stack. I was playing near the barn when Dad drove our International Harvester "M" into the yard, and trailing behind it was our stoneboat with Spike lying on it.

"What's the matter with Spike, Dad? Is he sick?"

"Albert ran over him with a load of hay. He can't walk."

"Will he get better?"

"I don't know. We'll have to see."

Spike lay in the corral next to the barn for a week. Every day, twice a day, Dad lifted Spike gingerly by his tail so as to take weight off Spike's damaged leg. Dad coaxed Spike to walk, but he cried in pain. On the eighth day, my uncle Bill showed up at our farm brandishing his .22-calibre rifle. I asked Dad what Bill was going to do, even though I knew.

"Go to the house," Dad said softly.

"I want to stay."

"Are you sure?"

"I want to be with Spike. He's my friend," I said, trying to make my tone sound as if Dad and Bill were traitors.

Spike lay in the middle of the corral, his golden front legs crossed in a relaxed pose. His panting made him appear to be smiling. Bill braced his rifle against the corral's board fence. I heard the shot and saw a spot of red form on Spike's forehead. His head hung in the air momentarily and then, as if being lowered by hydraulics, it eased itself onto his paws.

After supper I asked Dad where he was going as he was leaving the house. He turned back to me and said, "I'm going to take care of my friend." Dad buried Spike next to Grandpa Hulse's smokehouse.

After Spike died, we went through a series of farm dogs, several of which weren't smart enough to keep off U.S. Highway 83, which ran directly alongside our farmstead. Then I got Stub, whose markings—points of white on each foot, dabs of gold above each eye, a zigzag pattern of gold along his muzzle—were as perfectly paired as any I've ever seen. His only shortcomings were his four-inch tail and his fear of guns.

Just the sight of a gun sent Stub running for cover—even if the nearest available cover was our farmhouse. The first time Stub barged into our house, we were so surprised, we laughed, even though he ran all the way to Mom and Dad's bedroom. The second time he attempted entry, Mom's scolding voice stopped Stub at the entryway, as if her harshness and its echoing report were another type of firearm.

Conversely, no matter how cold the winter night and no matter how much Dad coaxed, Stub never willingly spent a night in the barn. But he was not without shelter.

During the holiday season, Dad constructed manger scenes out of straw bales, which he left in place for the remainder of the winter. At Christmastime, he placed two large spotlights to highlight all the plastic figures, many of which, kneeling, were three feet high. Because Dad and Mom were extravagant with their outdoor Christmas displays, carloads of sightseers routinely drove in a circle through our yard, and lying next to baby Jesus most nights was an eighty-pound canine ball covered with long black fur.

Stub was my unquestioning companion through seventh and eighth grades and through all of high school and college, until I betrayed him for a wife, a job in a city, and a basset hound named Tanya that not only came into our home but also slept with us. About a year after Nicki and I were married, Dad called and said Stub was sick. He had allowed himself to be shut up in the barn on the coldest nights, and he was getting thin. A few weeks later, Dad called and told me that Stub had eaten nothing but snow for a couple of days. His sentiment taking control, Dad then blubbered that Stub had not run away when he saw the rifle. Instead, he followed Dad from the front steps of the house toward the barn. About halfway, he sat and looked at Dad, gun in hand, as if to say, "This is far enough." And so it was. As soon as the frost was out of the ground, Dad buried Stub in a shady shelterbelt.

Along with studies on life and death, I also associate the barn with lessons about human behavior. For example, a few years after Uncle Bill shot Spike, I came to realize that he had been the perfect man for the job.

Dad had taught me how to set a gopher snare so I could "lasso" one around its midsection, and I had spent an entire morning trying to catch one. My weapon was a thirty-foot piece of baler twine, one end of which was fashioned into a hangman's noose that went around the perimeter of the hole. I moved from hole to hole, my patience diminishing after each attempt. Finally, I placed the snare around a hole on the edge of our pasture nearest our barn and told myself that if I didn't catch anything, I'd forget all about gopher hunting the old-fashioned way. I sat there for nearly a quarter of an hour, but no gopher appeared. In frustration, I turned toward the barn and yanked at the twine without looking at the hole. I felt a slight resistance, turned, and saw that I had snared a gopher by its neck instead of its midsection. My timing must have been split-second. My gopher was on a twine leash as if it were a pet. I tied the gopher to a post in the barn and went to dinner.

That afternoon Bill stopped by for a visit. I was walking my gopher in our yard when Bill pulled into the driveway. "What you got there?" he asked.

"It's a gopher I snared."

"How are you going to kill it?"

I hadn't considered killing the gopher. My plan was to have the gopher get used to me so I could pet it, perhaps keep it in the barn year-round (although I knew this was a risky plan because a similar scheme involving a pigeon hadn't worked out).

"You've got to kill it," Bill continued.

"I'll do it later," I said.

"Let's do it now. Let's drown it."

And with that, Bill snatched the twine from my hand and then led the gopher and me past our barn and out to the drainage ditch that wound through our pasture. At first he slowly weaved the gopher through the water, but it dog-paddled diligently. Then, he began dragging the animal through the water using a long, sweeping motion, faster and faster so that it stayed submerged. Afterward, he nonchalantly laid the muddy rodent at my feet and walked toward the house.

I never snared another gopher. Perhaps, stopping my snaring was what Bill had intended, but I doubt it. I think Bill confused toughness with mean-spiritedness. Regardless of his motivations, Bill's services as animal exterminator on our farm ended with that gopher's last watery breath.

A more complicated lesson about understanding and forgiveness took me longer to learn, and it involved Mom. When we had sheep, it was my job to bottle-feed the lambs whose mothers had died during birth. While it was fun to watch those black bundles of woolly energy jump and kick, it quickly became a chore to feed them. As the lambs sucked on the rubber-tipped soda pop bottles holding the warmed milk, their grassy mouths produced green foam that oozed along the bottle and onto my hands. The vomit-like smell of that acidic foam permeated and stained my skin and stubbornly resisted soap and hot water.

One afternoon, Mom told me it was time to feed the lambs. I was watching TV (possibly the Three Stooges) and pretended not to hear her call. She summoned me again, and still I resisted. The third time she called, her angry tone moved me, but as I was bending down to pull on my boots, the pressure caused a blood vessel in my nose to break. Nosebleeds were a recurring problem for me at that age, and so I wasn't surprised that Mom wasn't alarmed, even though my nose was pouring blood. But this time Mom forcefully stuffed tissue into the offending nostril and told me to get to the barn. I had pushed Mom too far. As a consequence, her temper had assumed a new dimension.

When Dad looked up from his chores and saw me standing there, crying, he said, "What are you doing out here, little man?"

"She made me come!" I screamed.

Calmly, he said, "Go back to the house."

As I was walking back, I looked down my nose and could see that the tissue outside my nostril was turning pink, an indicator, my experience told me, that the portion crammed into my nose was already blood-soaked. Back inside the house, and more subdued in front of Mom, I said, "Dad told me I didn't have to feed the lambs tonight."

As Mom was removing the soaked tissue and the attached blood clot from my nose, she told me I was spoiled. I felt betrayed, and Dad's taking my side, this time, provided inadequate comfort. Even years after I'd become an adult, years even after Dad had died, I couldn't conceive how Mom could have reached that hard-hearted conclusion. Why did she have to be so difficult, so scary, when I was young? The fact that Mom most likely had suffered from untreated depression wasn't enough to excite my compassion or ease my pain.

Not until I was well into my forties did I discover a way to reconcile Mom's hurtful behavior. My remedy has relied on another memory involving our barn. One of my preteen birthdays happened to coincide with a saturating spring rainfall that had turned our farmyard into a mud- and manure-filled swamp. Outside play was out of the question, but we still had the option of our haymow and games of hide-and-seek among the dwindling stack of hay and straw bales. However, the walk between house and barn and back again meant getting sneakers and blue jeans farm dirty. Mom's solution was to put on Dad's overshoes and carry my birthday guests one by one—on her back—to and from our barn. I imagine it was Mom's perfectionism propelling her that day, but it was the complexity of her spirit that I have come to accept as my present.

I cannot forget Mom's anger, symbolized by the day she insisted I feed the orphaned lambs when I had a bad nosebleed (a problem that eventually required cauterization of a blood vessel). But I must forgive that day, and others, because I, too, have let anger control me. One time was on a Mother's Day when Mom's ironic timidity kept her from asking her sister Ruth for a ride to the restaurant where we were going to eat dinner after church. Instead, I had to drive Mom to the restaurant and back to her home in her car because she was too arthritic to climb into my pickup truck. This round-trip added sixty miles to my travels that day (home to Fargo) and extended from five hours to six my car time, all of which I spent alone because Nicki had decided to spend a rare Mother's Day with her mom.

As Mom and I were driving to the restaurant, she began talking about her other sister, Goldie, who spent most of her golden years in Arizona (Goldie died in August 2008). Mom said my cousin Cathi, also an Arizona resident, was waiting on Goldie "hand and foot." At that moment, my desire to inflict emotional pain took on a presence I could feel, as if it were a finger, a hand, or my tongue, which I held, only because offering a guilt-edged response could change nothing. Instead, I exhaled, long and loud, in the hope that my nonverbal sarcasm flowed like water, washing over Mom and allowing realization to seep in. We drove on in silence, and I was uncharacteristically quiet throughout most of the dinner.

Less than a year later, Mom's first chemotherapy treatment shut down her poorly functioning kidneys, and I watched her continually vomit and gasp for breath. Mom and I spent much of her last day together, struggling, as we did that day in the barn when we saved the lamb. At times Mom grasped the bed rail as I once had clutched that wooden gate. All the while, I was sloughing off, like silk, the remainder of my bitterness about Mom's temper and harsh tongue that had clung to me since childhood.

About a year after Mom's death, Westhope celebrated its centennial, and this event put me in contact with Elaine Foltyn, the mother of twin boys, K–12 classmates of mine who were always present at my grade school birthday parties (and I at theirs). Elaine and her husband, Tony, had moved to Minot after he retired from the telephone cooperative, and so I hadn't seen Elaine for years. Our conversation quickly turned to Mom, and Elaine reminded me that she had been a member of the Westhope Garden Club for many years, as had Mom. Elaine stressed that none of those conversations about gardening was equal to the pleasant chat she'd had with Mom when she was hospitalized, about a week before she died. Elaine concluded our talk that day with these words: "I just want you to know that your Mom was really proud of you and Nicki."

That visit with Elaine has helped broaden my perspective. We no longer own the barn Dad built, but it nonetheless symbolizes one of my most precious lessons: the darkness and the light of human behavior are not exclusive, but additive. When I think of the barn now, my memory's eye sees the sun shining through black and blue storm clouds. And I hear snow geese singing, like happy children at play.

Big Boy Flies Solo Early; Touches Down Eventually (He Hopes)

I learned how to drive a car before I could ride a bicycle. My solo occurred when I was five or six in our salmon and white 1956 Oldsmobile. I certainly was large enough for this adventure. As proof, I offer one of Mom's sporadic entries in a journal designed to chronicle my childhood achievements: at age seven I stood fifty-two inches tall and weighed 126½ pounds. A big boy.

On the day I first drove that Olds, I imagine Dad asked, "Does Daddy's little man want to help?" Dad posed this question often.

"Yes." I wanted to help, to do well. To be good. I presume a farmer's practicality prompted Dad's decision regarding my first solo. Circumstances must have prevented another adult from driving the Olds home from Grandpa Trimble's farm, where we had gone to retrieve our one-ton Chevy pickup truck. Absent an adult, I became the perfect little man for the job.

I drove the Olds slowly out of Grandpa and Grandma Trimble's driveway, turned right onto the gravel road, and headed east into Westhope. The car's automatic transmission allowed me to focus only on steering and braking for the four-mile flight. I kept my eyes fixed on the road, the car's tires never once veering from the trail previous cars had made in the gravel. Once in a while, I peeked in the rearview mirror to check on Dad following behind in the pickup. I fretted about losing him in town, but with Dad in full view the entire time, I slipped along a couple of out-lying streets with ease: turning left, then right, then left again onto U.S. Highway 83. I headed north toward our farmstead. Once home, I jumped out of the car, sped into the house as fast as my fat legs could carry me, and in-formed Mom that I had helped. I had been good.

And Dad had been trusting, his hallmark. For the next decade and a half, he continued to be trusting, but his good intentions quickly began yielding unintended con-sequences. The year I turned eight, we had a run-in with our town's lone law enforcement officer, Louis Gerlach, a smiling, diminutive man perfectly sized for his patrol car, the town's only navy blue 1961 Ford Falcon. It was a cloudy Sunday in the spring, and Dad, my cousin Craig, and I were motoring slowly along an empty Main Street in our 1960 Olds, me at the wheel. Craig was in the front seat and Dad in the back. About two blocks from Craig's house, I noticed the Falcon following us. I reported the sighting to Dad, who told me to drive straight to Craig's house. Along the way, I displayed my best driving skills, as Craig and I weaved between giddiness and frenzy.

"Maybe he'll give me my driver's license."

"Nah, you've got to take some kind of test, don't you, Darrell?"

"Maybe he'll make an exception," I said, a hopeful tone rising in my voice. "Do you think he will, Dad? I bet he will."

"Maybe you'll have to go to jail," Craig said.

"Maybe you'll have to go to jail, too."

Dad wasn't saying much of anything. As soon as the Olds came to a complete stop in the vacant lot next to the

Harper house, Craig and I were on a dead run for the safety of his home. As Dad relayed to us about ten minutes later, Mr. Gerlach was quite impressed with my driving skills, but he nonetheless didn't approve of my driving in town, even with a chaperone.

So, our farm and the surrounding countryside became my Elba, where Dad and I, on occasion, used horsepower—the real thing—to propel ourselves across the landscape. Dad loved horses. He sold his last horse when he was seventy-one. Many times during our horseback rides, he reminded me how good a rider he was as a youngster—always remembering to retell the part about his being able to stand on the back of a horse going at a full gallop. Later on, when we got home and were sitting in our living room, I'd run my hand over the top of Dad's dented head, the result of his falling off a horse and landing headfirst on a rock. Blood flowed from his ears, he said. He was lucky to be alive.

My car-driving exploits in our 1965 Olds remained unchallenged by official law enforcement authorities, although Dad once conducted an unofficial inquiry into how I'd managed to knock the muffler off the car. When I was fourteen, Dad let me get a learner's permit. He no doubt was thinking I would help with more of the farmwork, but I was thinking I'd already learned quite a bit about raking hay, summerfallowing, and hauling grain. Having been duped into a false sense of maturity by farmwork, I felt ready for exploration, and automobiles were to be my mode of transport.

In December 1968, Dad broke his pattern of buying a new car every five years because our 1965 Olds, although white in color, had turned out to be a rusting lemon. I

don't know what prompted Dad and Mom to begin buying Oldsmobiles, but Dad's experience with our 1965
Olds didn't deter him from buying another Olds at a dealership in Bottineau. Even though that same dealer hadn't
resolved many of the mechanical shortcomings of our
1965 model. And even though the president of General
Motors didn't get on the line to speak with Dad the time
he called corporate headquarters to complain.

Our 1969 Olds—the big Olds—was a sporty two-door
with a factory-installed eight-track tape player. It also
came equipped with a 455-cubic-inch engine, and it had
a rocket ship emblazoned on the horn button in the center
of its sleek black steering wheel. A fitting symbol.

When I was fifteen and soon to be a sophomore in high
school, I attended a back-to-school party. Most of us were
drinking beer throughout, and when the party ended, I
decided to see how fast I could return home. My route was
a gravel road running between Antler, North Dakota, and
U.S. Highway 83. That big Olds handled beautifully. Even
at 115 mph, I felt as at ease as if I were sitting in Dad's
recliner watching *As the World Turns*. In fact, my feeling
of comfort and safety produced drowsiness, which caused
me to miss the turn. Almost. About three hundred yards
from the stop sign, I realized where I was, hit the brakes,
and went into a skid.

The car's momentum maintained a straightforward
direction, more or less, as it spun in a full circle, but by
the time the nose of the Olds was again beginning to point
in an easterly direction, the car's forward momentum
had slowed and an angular energy took over. The Olds
lurched into the south ditch about one hundred feet short
of the highway. As the car careened past the stop sign

(without hitting it), I regained my composure and took control of the Olds by tromping on the accelerator. We (the Olds and I now seemed bonded) shot out of the north–south ditch paralleling Highway 83 with tires squealing and grass and dirt flying. Within two minutes, I was walking into our house.

I thought my shortcut through a ninety-degree turn where gravel became pavement was my secret, but there was a witness: first-chair Todd, a trumpet-playing prodigy who likewise was returning home from the party. Before he went away to college that fall, Todd made sure I knew that he knew, and it was Todd's telling and retelling of my taillights-headlights-taillights maneuver that made my driving skills appear to be highly refined, at least in the minds of some, mine included.

Three months later I had more car trouble while coming back from a bar in Waskada, Manitoba, Canada. I was fifteen at the time. It wasn't much of an accident, really, one resulting only in a slightly noticeable dent behind the right front wheel well of that big Olds. In fact, Dad didn't notice the dent, but the next day he did want to know why bits of grass were stuck to the black vinyl on the interior panel of the driver's door. I told him I'd gotten stuck while turning around on a country road west of town, and I'd had little trouble getting out. He accepted my explanation and that was that.

But the truth was that I had left the U.S. port-of-entry station like a drag racer, headed for a dance in Westhope. That night, as the Olds idled on the U.S. side of the border, I saw by the car's clock that I had four minutes to cover the six miles to town if I wanted to arrive promptly at nine o'clock, when the dance was to begin. And so, I was off.

About two hundred yards from where I'd seen my green light, I slid that big Olds into a snow-filled ditch. The customs agent on duty loaned me a snow shovel, and I got the car out a little more than an hour later, with considerable help—in the form of grunting and shoving and slipping—from my teenage passengers, as well as another carload of underage drinkers, and potential dancers, returning Stateside from the same bar.

About a year later, I put that big Olds into a ditch full of spring runoff, all because of my first-love infatuation, who hailed from Newburg, North Dakota, a beautiful, popular, dark-haired cheerleader named Viva. More accurately, my problems originated with the ten or so beers I'd drunk to drown the pain of Viva's deciding to see other boys after we'd been dating for only a few months. The car didn't fare so well this time. By the time I tracked down someone with a pickup and a nylon rope, the engine had taken on water and refused to start. Fresh oil and a new filter, administered by a friend with mechanical skills, did no good. Nor did our attempts to push the Olds down a paved road at speeds of forty, sixty, and eighty miles an hour, respectively, and then once achieving each of those speeds, engaging the automatic transmission in hopes of getting the engine to fire.

I use the word *our* because after the dance we were all attending in Maxbass, North Dakota, had ended, my crisis drew quite a crowd (including Viva, for whom my predicament, I imagine, became a validation of her decision concerning our relationship). While the oil change was under way, the Maxbass cop dropped by and wrote up a friend for having an open container and for being a minor in possession of alcoholic beverages. By that time, all my beer was long gone and the events of the evening had sobered me up considerably—no incriminating evidence, except for the four individual skid marks that the odd angle of my slide into the ditch had produced. The proximity of a stalled car to skid marks adds up only to circumstantial evidence, and apparently there's no law against changing a car's oil and filter in the middle of nowhere. On this night, my punishment (besides knowing that I had brilliantly surpassed Viva's low expectations of me) was having to leave the Olds sitting on an approach and then explaining to Dad at two o'clock in the morning why we'd have to pull the car home the next day.

Standing in the doorway of my parents' bedroom, I whispered, "Dad? You awake?"

"Yeah." The answer came immediately out of the darkness.

"I had to leave the car in Maxbass tonight because it wouldn't start."

"What's wrong?"

"I'm not sure."

Dad, his easygoing manner at full bloom even during the dead of night, said, "We'll drive over after church tomorrow and pick it up."

I didn't tell Dad that a waterlogged engine was the most likely reason until we were actually in our pickup headed for Maxbass. This confession knocked a few petals off Dad's demeanor. We towed the car home, and on Monday a mechanic at the Farmers Union drained another quart and a half of water out of the engine, changed the points and spark plugs, and had the car running by late afternoon. The condition of the car was a topic of conversation at the service station and in school most of the day.

As I drove the stretch of U.S. Highway 83 that lay between town and home, my dread worked like a brake, keeping the 1969 Olds at about thirty miles an hour, about the same speed that 1956 Olds and I had moved more than a decade before. Supper that Monday night included Dad's brief lecture, not unlike past speeches, and, of course, Mom's scowls, which for years I'd been able to produce with activities much less grandiose than this caper.

Dad didn't ground me. In fact, he let me drive the Olds to Minot the following Saturday. My passengers were all Newburg girls (but not Viva). That sixty-mile drive to Minot must have been distance enough to expose a lingering mechanical trauma, because at one of our first stoplights, I noticed a peculiar odor. It turned out that water had seeped through seals into the car's transmission, too. Instead of a healthy pinkish hue, the transmission fluid, registering about a half inch above the full mark on the dipstick, was an ugly, foamy gray brown. The following Monday the Olds was back in the shop getting its transmission drained, a two-day job.

That big 1969 Olds was Dad's last. Unlike the 1965 Olds, the big Olds had performed as designed, but I had aged it prematurely. Dad's choice for a replacement was a 1972 Dodge Charger with a speedometer registering 150 mph. I didn't wreck the Charger until I was in college. But before I became the designated driver of that machine, I wheeled around as a high school senior and then a college freshman in a 1968 Ford Torino equipped with a 390-cubic-inch engine (and all the potential for driving disaster that such displacement implies).

I was a second-semester freshman when I snugged the Torino up against a telephone pole. Left front fender and headlight assembly. A friend and I were coming back from a bar in East Grand Forks, Minnesota, and I accelerated from a stoplight too quickly, hit a patch of ice, and lost control of that poorly engineered Torino. The car's rear end was simply too light; the slightest veer set it skidding. My passenger and I reached these conclusions as we munched on Grinders at the Red Pepper, about two blocks from the accident scene. Judging the damage to be less than five hundred dollars, I didn't report the Torino accident, but I did reflect on how the big Olds and I could have handled the situation. The next morning, I called Dad. That night, he called me to say that his insurance agent said not reporting the accident had been the right thing to do.

I drove the Torino home on Easter weekend, and, coincidentally, the first person I met when I pulled into town was the car's previous owner. Driving toward me, he motioned for me to stop. We talked briefly from idling vehicles. I felt bad for him because I could tell he felt bad, as if he'd lost a friend: he'd bought the Torino new, his first car. I repeated my rationalization, told him the Torino was just poorly engineered—too light in the ass end. When we pulled away, I imagine he was thinking about the Torino. I was thinking about the big Olds.

Dad decided I should drive the Charger back to college to finish out the school year. Although not the same vintage as the Charger featured in the movie *Bullitt*, our Dodge nonetheless was a sleek-looking car that could turn heads. Four heads certainly turned one rainy Friday night. I was double-dating with Tim, the former star of a hapless high school football team from Sherwood, North Dakota. Tim and I had been gridiron competitors, but now we lived on the same dormitory wing. His date was a high-school-turned-college sweetheart. Mine was a delightful-looking blind date, still a senior in high school, a friend of Tim's date. We were coming back from a sorority party at a bar, and the backseat couple was snuggling. Not wanting to miss out, I decided a little on-the-go kissing with my date couldn't hurt. I was thinking differently after the Charger failed to negotiate a curve in the road, one that my eyes easily would have registered if they had been fixed on the road. Because the road's shoulder was so narrow, I had no time to react before the Charger sideswiped the guardrail, an impact forceful enough to reconfigure the car's entire right side.

The Charger was still drivable after the collision, and so we decided to stop at a twenty-four-hour breakfast place to talk out our strategy. Yes, alcohol again had been involved in this fiasco, but none of us was really drunk, at least not by the more lax definition of the time. Even so, none of us wanted to visit the police station, so when I suggested that our accident was perpetrated by someone else—someone who had *hit and run*—we had consensus.

The next day being a Saturday, I spun my yarn for the police and Dad. The following Monday, well practiced now, I told the tale to a claims adjuster. Of course, Dad's insurance company still had to pay the bill, but I had managed to assume a victim's status.

I drove home from college in early May with the Charger already back from the body shop and looking as if it were brand new. Dad had Uncle Cliff scout around for a used fender for the Torino, but Cliff couldn't find one, and if Cliff couldn't scavenge one, no one would. Because the Torino had too many miles to bother fixing it with new parts, Dad traded in the car, as is, on a 1974 Ford LTD for Mom and him and then passed the Charger on to me.

The last time I smacked the Charger, most of my friends truly thought it was the other guy's fault. In fact, they agreed with me that it was probably because I was such a good driver that the accident even occurred. It happened during a March blizzard on a Saturday. In the morning, we headed out early to stock up on booze for the blizzard party. The visibility was so poor that Terry, my companion when I smacked the Torino and the person now riding shotgun, had to stick his head out of the passenger-side window to guide me along the outlying city street we were traveling. (Terry was an accounting major at a school known for turning out top-rated accountants, and so I trusted his judgment implicitly.) After getting our supplies, we even managed to weave our way through a traffic jam that later turned out to be a news-making seventeen-car pileup. We were back in the dorm, with no incidents to report, about two hours after we had left.

Of course, we eventually drank all the alcohol, and three of us volunteered to be couriers of more. I was once again piloting the Charger. The storm had subsided by then, but cold high-pressure air filled the void. Anxious to return with the booty, I began the drive with fogged-up windows. We turned right onto the narrow north–south street that ran along the coed dormitory, and we had proceeded only about 150 yards when someone yelled, "Dean, car!"

Thinking I'd ventured into the oncoming lane of traffic, I automatically swerved the Charger to the right—right into the back of a car that was illegally parked on the street. The impact actually pushed the other car up against a "No

Parking Anytime" sign planted in the boulevard about thirty feet south of the entrance for the North Dakota State School for the Blind. I must have had the Charger traveling about fifteen to twenty miles an hour, because the impact propelled the three of us forward with considerable force. "Doc," a 250-pound New Yorker from Queens whose grade point average dissolved his dream of becoming a commercial airline pilot, had called shotgun, and his head (and weight) created an intricate spider web in the windshield. Terry, seated in the middle, used his forehead to break off the rearview mirror (the impact of which produced a pair of black-and-blue eyes that for about a week oddly complemented his blond hair). I used my knees to make two dents, almost perfectly round, in the metal dash. Exterior damage to the Charger included both front fenders and the grill.

Doc and Terry walked back to the dorm and informed the partyers, and someone summoned the police. Terry then went to the emergency room for several stitches. After the cop arrived at the scene, he and I waited for nearly twenty minutes before the owner of the illegally parked car showed up. Tracked down at Frenchy's, a popular college bar, the owner came with his brother, who I found out later was captain of the university's debate team. While the three of us sat in the back of the police cruiser discussing the situation, the brother who owned the parked car actually got out of the squad car once and puked, an action I thought should vindicate me. I thought wrongly. I was cited for failure to have a motor vehicle under control. My fine was twenty dollars, which after driving my wrecked Charger the few blocks to the police station, I paid in person that same evening.

It was after this accident that Dad and his insurance company began to take my driving habits seriously. What angered Dad the most about this incident was the threat from his insurance company—a company he'd done business with for thirty years. Dad's agent told him that if he didn't drop me from his policy, they'd have to drop Dad. When the agent found out that I was getting married that summer and soon to be fending for myself in the auto insurance world, he agreed to keep Dad's policy in force. And so, Dad's anger with me quickly subsided, as usual.

Marriage and the aging process (not necessarily synonymous with the maturing process in my case) seem to have cured my propensity to crash cars into other cars (with the exception of a few embarrassments I've managed in my own driveway). And so, for much of my married life with Nicki, I looked back upon my driving incidents through the eyes of someone having come of age during the 1970s—that is, I was thankful I hadn't killed myself or anyone else, but beyond the slight remorse accompanying this thankfulness, I was amused. Because I'd not been the perpetrator of any serious physical injury, I felt absolved, almost as if I were a medal-decorated veteran of the Wild Oats War and therefore entitled to tell my tales.

One story I took particular joy in telling involved the Charger. While alcohol was always our drug of choice in high school, my friends and I could, if we were determined enough, find other drugs to consume as well. Marijuana and hashish were our favorites. Once I was in college, pot smoking became routine. And once when some friends and I were smoking pot in the Charger, a joint I had just rolled and set on the dash subsequently rolled down into the defroster vent. I wasn't all that concerned because we still had plenty of pot, and I thought the joint would dry up or get ground up by the blower motor.

But my run-in with that parked car in front of the School for the Blind caused me to fret while the Charger was in the body shop. The repairs involved removing parts of the dash. When I got the car back with no comment, I immediately assumed the repairman had found the joint and helped himself. This seemed a logical conclusion to me because I had convinced myself that almost everybody smoked pot.

About three months after I got the Charger back— about a year to the day the joint had rolled into the vent— my friend Dave and I were driving somewhere when he started getting pelted in the face. Somehow, that joint had worked its way through the Charger's ductwork and was trying to come out—intact—except for what hit Dave's face.

Dave and I had been friends since grade school and had roomed together during college. Much of our, and other friends', recreational time had been spent devising ways to smoke pot or hashish with materials on hand or readily accessible. Tinfoil had become a trusted tool. For example, after once discarding a wad of tinfoil a group of us thought we no longer needed, we drove back several hours later to the spot on the country road where we'd tossed it out the window. Despite its being a windy evening, the tinfoil still lay where it had come to rest, and so we quickly retrieved it, uncrumpled it, and smoked more hash. We were pioneers of recycling, I suppose. On the day the joint decided to present itself to us, Dave simply used chewing gum jammed onto a ballpoint pen to extract it, and then we smoked it, even though it was only nine o'clock in the morning.

A few years after I'd graduated from college, I came to know one of Dave's first cousins, Jerry, whose sweet tooth is legendary and whose "lunch" while dieting might consist of two spoonfuls of jam. When Jerry got married (just a few years shy of turning fifty), he took me aside during the reception and told me there was someone who wanted to meet me. Then he introduced me to Kathy, a first cousin on his father's side. Actually, it was a reintroduction: Kathy was the blind date I had some twenty years earlier, the night I sideswiped the guardrail with the Charger.

The passing of more than two decades had done little to affect Kathy's eyes and her smile, which in tandem worked like a beacon, filling in my shadowy memories of our one-night encounter. She smiled often and was pleasant, and our conversation was enjoyable. As it turns out, she went to another college after high school and took up social work. The few minutes Kathy and I spent together at the wedding reception made me feel young, and shallow. During all the years I've known Jerry, I'm sure that I must have mentioned the incident involving the Charger and the guardrail. But I never once thought that my blind date might be Jerry's cousin because I'd forgotten her name.

Like an unexpected gift, that gorgeous young girl turned gracious middle-aged woman helped me understand how my recklessness had damaged much more than plastic and metal and flesh and bones. By the time I'd become reacquainted with Kathy, Dad was dead, and so, my taking lightly the trust he placed in me became another addition to my list of regrets. I've since wondered how many irretrievable hours, minutes—seconds—I have callously disregarded.

When I was home visiting Mom a year or two before she died, I noticed a 1969 Olds parked by the side of a Quonset on a farmstead south of Westhope. The Olds was a two-door, bearing the same champagne-gold coloring as the big Olds we owned. I have fantasized several times about buying that car, or another Olds of similar vintage, especially since General Motors has phased out its Oldsmobile division.

But no. Enough wheel spinning.

Haunted

orth Dakota's tuberculosis sanatorium seemed just as creepy to me when I was in high school, and even later, as it did when I was four. Grandpa Hulse, my uncle Cliff, his son Craig, and another uncle, Neil, all received treatment for TB at San Haven, "the San," a fortress in the war against what at one time was a deadly physical disease. However, this well-intentioned institution—this city on a hill—provided little defense against emotional traumas manifesting as human weaknesses.

When Dad's mom died of TB in 1920, the disease went by a different name: consumption, to describe how its victims wasted away. I, too, contracted this highly contagious disease when I was a preteen, probably as a result of my exposure either to Grandpa or Cliff, but I was one of the fortunate few who avoided hospitalization because my immune system was able to fight off the disease. The only physical evidence of my TB experiences is a scarred lung.

In 1972 our family physician recommended that Dad, Mom, and I receive TB medication on an outpatient basis, as a precaution, due to Craig's bout with TB a year earlier. And so, whenever we ran out of isoniazid, white horse pills we were to take daily for a year, I picked up refills. I rocketed along in our 1969 Oldsmobile: south on U.S.

Highway 83, and then east, mostly, on state Highway 5. This one-hundred-mile round-trip seldom took me longer than eighty or ninety minutes, including my stop at the San.

Along that course the farm fields, infrequent pastures, and unnatural shelterbelts dip only on occasion, a reminder to drivers that a glacier once ironed the Souris River Valley. And off in the distance, always, Turtle Mountain. Hills really, this range straddles the U.S.–Canada border along the forty-ninth parallel and extends, from east to west, not more than forty miles before abruptly stopping about twenty-five miles east of Westhope. The grasses of Turtle Mountain sparkle with windblown shades of green during the spring and in wet summers, as do the trees, mostly paper birch. But throughout many summers and in the fall, the semiarid climate produces the illusion that the hills are stacks of fawn-speckled turtles.

The San sat atop a crest on Turtle Mountain, north of Dunseith alongside U.S. Highway 281. This location offered a higher altitude, compared to other spots in North Dakota, and thus thinner air, which could help arrest a person's TB, although oxygen-poorer air promised no cure. From a distance, the San oozed eeriness: an institutional complex with buildings of brick, fieldstone, or stucco, a water tower, and evergreens, visible for perhaps ten miles.

On my trips for pills, I wasted no time at Dale's Café in Dunseith, where Mom, Dad, and I often had eaten meals after visiting Grandpa Hulse. Instead, I slipped through Dunseith as fast as the city speed limit allowed and then devoured those remaining few miles on 281, winding higher and higher in a northeasterly direction past rural homes, some crying for paint, and past yards sheltering abandoned cars. I followed the San's familiar curving entrance for a quarter mile or so. Evergreens to my left. On my right, I passed by the multivehicle fieldstone garage, several buildings that looked like dorms, and a few small houses. The evergreens eventually opened into the park where Mom and I had walked when Grandpa was a patient. Finally, I reached the circular driveway and parking lot in front of the hospital.

When I try to recall the hospital lobby, I see nothing but dim tungsten lights throwing a golden transparency around the room and onto a display case, prominent, as is the registration desk at hotels. Inside the case were handicrafts that I presumed patients had made. The office where I picked up our pills was somewhere off the main lobby, but close by. The sounds of heels on tile are not a powerful recollection, but then, I made it a point to be quick about my business because my family's history with this place produced an aura that pressed against my chest.

When Grandpa Hulse lived with us, he and I shared a bedroom and a bed. I remember my orange and white phonograph and its yellow vinyl records that were small in diameter, like forty-fives, but had a smaller center hole like an LP. In the mornings, "Casey Jones" was a favorite tune I played for Grandpa as he was putting on his familiar gray work shirt and matching pants over his wool long underwear, which he wore year-round. He could slip on his pants while sitting in a chair, a feat that still amazes me, mostly because I can't understand why he thought it was a skill that needed mastering.

Grandpa also smoked, but only outside—Mom's orders—which meant he smoked seasonally. He favored

Parliament cigarettes, the brand featuring a recessed filter. Half a cigarette in the morning and the other half in the afternoon. As he smoked, I sat in a lawn chair next to his.

Grandpa contracted TB in October of 1959, but there were drugs for treating the disease then, so his stay at the San lasted only until July 1960, two months after I'd turned five. During that time, the only visiting I did with him was on warm fall days, again in the spring, and then summer, through an open window in his room, because regulations forbade young children to enter the hospital.

The Christmas that Grandpa spent at the San had to be when my cousin Beverly and her husband gave me a toy machine gun because I don't recall ever receiving another Christmas present from her. I still have a photo of the white artificial Christmas tree we used before going natural, and nestled underneath this fake tree is the box with blue and gold wrapping paper that I recall as being the one concealing the gun.

As an adult, I have listened to taped interviews from an oral history project involving the San. One person giving an interview worked as a baker at the San for many years and spoke of how Christmas lights covered all the evergreens, and how the dining room featured a Christmas tree and candles on every table the entire month of December. This setting was so pretty that some of the workers invited guests up to the San for the Christmas Eve meal.

My early memories of the San include a brick wall at the end of a long grass walkway, shade trees aplenty, and benches dotting the park. And I remember names: Johnny, Grandpa's roommate, his hair black, his face featureless; and Walnut Crush, a ten-cent candy bar in an orange wrapper that Grandpa once threw to me.

When I accompanied Mom and Dad to the San, Dad went to Grandpa's room, and Mom stayed with me. I ran ahead of Mom to a familiar spot on the lawn and began yelling, "Grandpa. Grandpa." My greetings often drew the attention of other patients who were gazing out their windows, no doubt wondering when they could go home. The day Grandpa came home, I got to the wall and yelled, "Grandpa," but Johnny appeared instead.

"Your Grandpa's not here," he said.

"Where is he?"

Johnny merely pointed toward the entrance of the hospital. I turned and saw Grandpa, suitcase in hand, standing in the circular driveway next to our car. I was too excited to turn back and say good-bye to Johnny. I ran toward our car without ever taking my eyes off Grandpa. It rained on the way home that day, a thunderstorm featuring a blue-black sky. Like noisy rainbirds, the weather perhaps was a harbinger itself because Grandpa died that fall from heart failure.

Uncle Cliff became a patient at the San in the early 1960s when he was in his forties. He smoked packs of Winstons every day but quit smoking at the San. Like mine, Cliff's immune system had fought the disease, so his two-month stay was a precaution against recurrence.

But even if Cliff's TB had been active, he wouldn't have been confined to bed because the drug treatment available to him had made complete bed rest as outmoded as other, more hideous treatment methods. Cliff once told me that predrug treatment often involved using unheated cottages, where patients with active TB resided year-round, regardless of how harsh the North Dakota winters got. Mittens, several layers of blankets, and hot water bottles were all part of the "sleepwear" for these cottage dwellers.

While a patient, Cliff fought boredom by making leather crafts, as generations of previous patients had done. He made me a coin purse of blond leather, which I still have, tucked away in a dresser drawer. Cliff also passed time at the San by walking up to the infirmary's roof and gazing toward the barns, which sat east of the hospital and were still in use in the 1960s. The San had been designed to be self-sustaining, a small town, of sorts. The property included about six hundred acres of land for raising crops and livestock. The San eventually had its own ZIP code.

By the time my cousin Craig received treatment for TB at the San in 1971, there were fewer than a handful of TB patients. Craig had a five-bed ward all to himself. The majority of hospital rooms and staff were devoted to the care of developmentally disabled residents (known universally then as the mentally retarded). These patients were the so-called overflow from the state school in Grafton.

Craig stayed at the San for less than a month and could leave on weekends. On Sundays, I drove him back to the San from Cliff's nearby cabin at Lake Metigoshe. Taking a tree-tunneled gravel road east from the lake, we intersected U.S. Highway 281 several miles north of the San. The first time I drove him back, Craig directed me to a road on the property I'd never noticed before, one that took us to the back of the hospital, where we could enter unobserved and take the stairs, unseen, to Craig's north-facing ward.

Craig passed some of his time at the San by focusing his attention on the disabled patients. Somehow, Craig had acquired syringes, which he filled with water and smuggled to the hospital roof. As the patients were enjoying sunshine at picnic tables near the same spot where I had visited with Grandpa Hulse, Craig directed streams of water onto unsuspecting heads. I witnessed the procedure and then took part in it. There were startled jerks, hands moving quickly to wet heads, and looks toward the sky. Our victims located us, smiled, and waved. Craig and I waved back, and through this exchange I developed the misguided notion that I was actually doing those patients a favor—that cruel attention is a form of kindness.

Shortly after Craig returned home from the San, the clutch went out of Cliff's Opel station wagon, the vehicle I had used to drive Craig to the San. Cliff blamed Craig. Craig pointed a finger at me. All I knew was that I was finished leaving the San at dusk.

One of Mom's photo albums contains snapshots of the San, black-and-white images showing a sunken rock garden and a lily pond, implying a country club setting. Mom couldn't remember who took the photos, so I'm left to presume it might have been someone visiting Neil Rosendahl, the husband of my aunt Myrtle, Dad's sister.

Neil died six years before I was born. I've seen only one picture of Neil, his wedding photo, in which he's positioned behind Myrt, whose flapper-style bob is becoming and whose face shows none of the physical wear that the anxiety and hard work of her later life produced. The lapels of Neil's suit coat are wide enough to accommodate two boutonnieres, and the part in his shiny, slicked hair is as straight as a good farmer's furrow. The couple's eyes appear focused on the same object, their vision of the future perhaps. Because this static wedding photo perpetually lives in the present tense, the imaginary couple will forever be acting out a tragic dramatic irony.

I've heard several stories about Neil and Myrt. For instance, Mom told me once that Dad thought Neil could be moody. Maybe so, but I bristled when hearing Mom use the word *moody* to describe him. I've been treated for depression, and I don't believe I could have lived as Neil did. He was a patient at the San for eleven years, from 1938 until 1949. He underwent various treatments. The most grisly of these procedures was the surgical removal of ribs, a few at a time, in the hope that this surgery (a routine practice before drugs) could collapse infected portions of a lung and thereby halt the spread of TB.

Neil suffered in other ways, too. His children, Beverly and Garnet, were three and five, respectively, when he entered the San, and as they grew to be fourteen and sixteen, the only means they had of talking with him was through a second-story window, similar to how I visited later with Grandpa Hulse. But Beverly and Garnet's conversations were different from mine because Neil was bedridden: limited to talking and pursuing other activities requiring only the use of his hands, such as woodworking. Beverly, now dead, told me of the hours she spent roaming the grounds of the San. She offered no specific details of scenery, just the vague sense of perpetual motion. *Aimless* is a word that popped into my head while she talked. I missed my opportunity to ask Garnet about his memories before he died because we were separated by several states for much of his life, and I didn't feel I knew him well enough to bring up sensitive subjects.

When I helped Beverly move to a different apartment more than half a century after her dad died, she still possessed one of his intricate assemblages composed of matchstick-sized pieces of wood. Although I can't recall its exact form, I do remember thinking about its function—that is, its ability to collect dust.

Of course, Neil's isolation during those years also meant no conjugal contact with Myrt, who had a child about halfway through his hospitalization. Mom said she and Dad never spoke about Myrt's situation, but Mom did come to learn of a frank conversation that Myrt and Neil had in his anything-but-private hospital ward. Mom remembered only Myrt's line: "Can't you see I'm pregnant?"

I can only imagine how Neil might have responded. Perhaps silent dignity was what he clung to.

I've often wondered what the worst part of Neil's sentence at the San was. Certainly, the lack of contact with his children was stressful, although divorce might create a similar separation. Likewise, infidelity causes heartache, but it is not uncommon. Perhaps the traumas of repeated surgeries and a useless, sedentary life forced on a man in his thirties, then his forties. No. What stands out in my mind as the water torture of Neil's years at the San (and Myrt's at home) is the utter relentlessness of their lives. Eleven helpless years resulting from an irony of infection: if Neil had become ill only a decade later than he did, he again would have walked with his wife and his children. Free.

The obituary announcing Neil's death appeared on the front page of my hometown newspaper, the *Westhope Standard*, on Thursday, June 16, 1949. Among the mourners listed were his two children, Beverly and Garnet, but not their half brother, Richard (Dick) Rosendahl. For this occasion there is another family anecdote: either Beverly or Garnet supposedly said, "My dad died today." Dick replied, "Mine didn't."

No longer called consumption, TB is a bacterial disease primarily affecting the lungs, but it can attack other organs. Craig's TB, for instance, was in a kidney. Without diagnosis or drug treatment, people suffering from pulmonary TB may cough up deadened portions of their lungs, and so the disease is still dangerous, although it no longer poses the threat to Americans it once did.

The San has not served TB patients since 1973, and in the 1980s, a class-action lawsuit allowed many of North Dakota's developmentally disabled citizens to leave the San and live in communities across the state. In the summer of 2001, I drove through the San, by then owned by the Turtle Mountain Band of Chippewa (Ojibwe). I followed the familiar curving entrance for a quarter mile or so past the evergreens. On the right I passed the fieldstone garage, its roof now collapsed. Windows were missing in the buildings that looked like dorms, as well as in the small houses. In fact, every window was missing from every building I could see, broken out by vandals or removed by scavengers. Graffiti covered the hospital's brickwork. The unkempt park where Mom and I had walked when Grandpa Hulse was a patient seemed smaller, as did the circular driveway in front of the hospital. Bricks and broken glass littered the driveway, a scene reminding me of a bomb blast. A few months after my visit, a teenage boy fell down an abandoned elevator shaft in the hospital and died, probably the same elevator Craig and I avoided when he was a patient there. A news account reports that many youth in the area believe the San is haunted.

Skeletons in the closet. Ghosts in the machine. Guilty skeleton-ghosts search among the rubble of sad memories at the San. Graceful rainbows appear other places, other times.

An Agrarian Gift

In the late 1960s, our oat crop got hit by rust, a fungal disease that can devastate cereal grain. We were lucky. We had some oats left to harvest. When I swathed those oats, my arms, my clothes, and our swather itself were coated with a reddish brown powder at day's end. Blowing my nose yielded auburn mud.

Disease was only one among a plague of discouragements for Dad on our farm: thirty-minute downpours that made lakes of fields, drowning plants and hopes; drought and relentless, mocking wind that turned our coarse soil into dust and black beaches where nothing grew except despair; grasshoppers with pincerlike mouths that scythed maturing grain heads; unseasonable cold that shut off plants' life flow like a hand to a faucet.

Unmanageable unknowns are a commodity that farmers get in abundance. In this respect, farming is both unique and unalterable, and as such, it requires the commitment of an artist who seeks payment in kind more often than remuneration. Despite nature's disastrous assertions, my dad was one of those artists. Another was Sam Lykken.

I don't know whether Lykken had any truck with the art world and the abstractions and intangibles therein. I never met him. I trust that through all the burdens and benefits of being on the land he became thoroughly a part of it—through all the sweat and fatigue, the feelings of fear and doubt, of determination and satisfaction. I do know this much: he produced a masterpiece of generosity, one affecting generations of barley farmers.

In 1992 I was working as a reporter for a regional farm publication. On a tip from a university researcher, plant pathologist Brian Steffenson, I set up an interview with Sam Lykken's sons, Percy, the eldest, and Sam Jr. Steffenson wanted to speak to Lykken's sons and to see the site of their father's discovery. I was impressed by Steffenson's respect for the elder Lykken (dead for decades) and his miraculous contribution to agriculture. Also, I was curious about what his sons, neither of whom farmed, had to say about their father. We met at the former Lykken farmstead, about three miles east of Kindred, North Dakota.

Lykken's sons told us that their father was a meticulous man. Even though by the mid-1930s he used his tractor for plowing, disking, and harrowing, he parked it and hitched up the horses when it came time to plant. Sam Jr. said, "He was very, very fussy about planting."

While soil compaction might have been a concern, Sam Lykken could have had other reasons for relying on horsepower. Regardless of his reasons, the result was this: planting took him extra time. And so, the sight that greeted Sam Lykken during a rust epidemic in the mid-1930s must have been particularly disheartening. A barley crop next to the Lykken farmstead was rusted out, stricken before the plants had headed and therefore unharvestable. Because the twenty-acre field lay alongside the lane running out to the county road, Sam Lykken's eastward view as he drove to and from church on a particular summer Sunday was one of stunted yellow, orange, and brown plants. To someone like me, a farm boy influenced by the 1970s, the scene might have prompted a comparison with a sculptured shag carpet displaying brilliant earth tones. What Sam Lykken was thinking that Sunday will forever be a mystery. But his routine remained recognizable. After dinner, he went for a walk to check the fields— even his rusted barley field, where, with an average yield (according to agronomist estimations), there should have been about twelve or thirteen million healthy barley plants. Instead of seeing millions or hundreds of thousands or even tens of thousands of healthy barley plants, Sam Lykken found one, standing in the midst of devastation, an agent of salvation. The day he discovered his healthy green plant, he encircled it with a fence made of coarse screening.

Sam Jr. said, "I remember how excited he was because we all had to go out and look at it."

Why did Sam Lykken bother walking through his field that day? A casual observer could conclude quickly that Lykken's crop was a lost cause. But he did walk into that field. I think he went because he was an artist. In looking at the crop, he was looking at himself.

During my interview, the nonfarming Lykken boys spoke of their experiences on the farm without implication. They told of hauling water to keep six hundred Chinese elms alive through a summer when grasshoppers flourished instead of crops. I could imagine the muscle-burning pain of hauling pails of murky water up the Sheyenne River's steep, hot, mosquito-infested bank. Their chores and their challenges echoed stories of thousands of farm boys who've gone on to greener pastures since the 1930s, the decade when North Dakota's farm population peaked.

With guilt still in his voice, the younger Sam Lykken also told of his neglectfulness with a stubborn lawn-mower, and the resulting tall grass that attracted their cattle. "Dad planted the barley he'd saved in our garden," he said. "The cows got into the garden once and almost ruined it. I know it set him back a year."

In 1992 I stood alongside Sam Lykken's sons in what had been their father's famous barley field. As rainfall spotted our jackets and their eyeglasses after a year-long drought, I read in the Lykkens' expressions a mixture of regret and relief, probably because that is how I often feel about having left the farm. Farmers and ex-farmers, it seems, are co-dependent, constantly grappling with the mixed emotions produced by living with, or having divorced, a cantankerous, consuming lover.

Retired when I met him, Sam Jr. had run a successful farm machinery business. Selling farm equipment isn't that far afield from farming, but far enough to offer a degree of certainty impossible for farmers. But then, one needs to consider the uncertain rewards of farmers. The single barley plant that Sam Lykken nurtured to maturity yielded eighteen kernels. Sam Jr. said, "I distinctly remember him shelling it out at the kitchen table."

Eventually, Sam Lykken offered some of the barley he'd grown to agronomists at the North Dakota Agricultural College, now North Dakota State University, to use for testing and breeding. When the refined barley became available to upper midwestern farmers during the 1940s, it carried the name *Kindred*, Lykken's hometown.

There were four rust epidemics in the 1950s, but damage to the region's barley crop was negligible. Steffenson, the plant pathologist, explained that what made Kindred special was its "T-gene," which enabled resistance to the wheat stem rust fungus that attacks both wheat and barley. The fungus constantly adapts to its environment and eventually overcomes a plant's defenses. But decades later, the Kindred T-gene still helps protect upper midwestern barley varieties.

Lykken's selection of what became Kindred barley has to be the most significant contribution to barley production in the Upper Midwest during the twentieth century, Steffenson said. He stressed, "Farmers will not obtain good yields or malt quality unless there is rust protection in the varieties they grow. The savings to growers must have been in the hundreds of millions of dollars."

Lykken's contribution to his neighbors and their children who went on to farm rests on his decision to walk through a barley field that was decimated, percentage-wise, a hundredfold, minus the smallest yet most significant fraction imaginable. I wasn't able to see what Lykken did, but I did watch Dad, and in the spring his decisions on which crops to plant were guided many times by the need of the land, not desire for more money. Having seen wind remove topsoil down to the hardpan in the 1930s, Dad always erred on the side of conservation. And so, even though a particular field had been in summer-fallow the season before and therefore had the nutrients to support a wheat crop, Dad might nonetheless decide to plant a less-profitable crop, oats, which can produce an abundance of straw and provide the knolls in a soil-black field extra erosion-preventing residue.

Even though Dad was no hometown hero, he had the soul of a Lykken-style farmer. I have a small spiral-bound notebook in which Dad recorded oil changes on our tractors. At the top of one page is written, "5-3-78," two days before my twenty-third birthday, and below, this entry: "All is well once more. Dean and Nicki are take-ing [sic] over the farm. We had a good crop last year."

I also have images of Dad put to memory: one, from 1992, the year he died, when he was coping with the after-math of a massive heart attack. Seated in his wheelchair, Dad was shaving with his rechargeable razor. As he was finishing, he ran his right hand across his face to check for smoothness, and then he let it wander down across atro-phied shoulder and chest muscles (he once had a forty-six-inch chest). He examined the sagging skin hanging on his torso, then looked up at me, smiled, and said, "It looks like I need to be ironed."

I farmed for only two years before quitting. A reason for my quitting I settle on frequently is this: I did not in-herit Dad's optimism.

Years after Sam Lykken died, military technology spawned the global positioning system (GPS), which now provides progressive farmers with details such as yield and fertility data. Proponents have coined a phrase: site-specific farming. But what would a GPS map of Lykken's rusted-out barley field have revealed? A bulletin produced in 1999 by the North Dakota State University Extension Service begins with this sentence: "Site-specific farming is a different way of thinking about the land." When I pre-tend that Lykken and Dad have read that sentence, I see their lips form knowing smiles.

Avon Calling

O f all the times Eleanore Ledoux came calling on Mom as the Avon lady, my memory homes in on a harsh moment during the summer of 1968 when I was thirteen. I had been cultivating about a mile from home when the alternator on our 5010 John Deere tractor went kaput. I drove home to call Dad, who was in town, because I didn't yet have a learner's permit and driving into town would have risked my getting a ticket.

When I pulled into our yard, I recognized the burgundy and white Ford Galaxie 500 parked in our driveway. The huge cars that Eleanore's husband, Hank, preferred were not a good match for Eleanore's diminutive frame.

Based on years of eyewitness experience, I knew that when Mom saw the Ledoux car rolling into our yard, she probably muttered angrily, "Oh, darn that Eleanore. Why is she stopping today, of all days?" I also expected Mom to have calmed down by the time Eleanore had reached our doorstep. In fact, by the time it took our community's tiny Avon lady to remove herself from the shadow of the car's steering wheel and hoist her sample case from her car, Mom could be trusted to have put on the coffeepot and plated her goodies.

After I had explained the tractor breakdown to Mom and Eleanore, I dialed the number of the Gateway Hotel, where I knew Dad was taking a coffee break in the café.

As the telephone rang, I noticed the mound of peapods lying on the kitchen counter next to the sink and deduced which component of Mom's morning busyness Eleanore's visit had postponed. While I talked with Dad, Mom and Eleanore continued their conversation, and as I was hanging up the telephone's receiver, I heard Eleanore say, "I've never seen Dean with a dirty face."

Eleanore's sarcasm hit me like a slap. I don't remember whether Mom had a reply. Shame and anger had taken control of my imagination. As Eleanore sat in our kitchen sipping coffee and nibbling at a seven-layer bar, I saw her calling on neighbors, gossiping about her experiences in our home, past and present, and I feared her loose talk could unjustly saddle me, or already had, with a reputation for being slothful.

To my mind, Eleanore's criticism implicated me in Dad's decision, which, when I was a toddler, had been to enroll most of our farm in the Soil Bank, a ten-year government program aimed at idling land. In return, willing farmers such as Dad received fixed annual payments. The program's goal was to reduce commodity supplies and thereby raise prices. From listening in on other visits, I knew what Mom and Eleanore thought of oddball loafers such as Ole and Herman Haugen, real-life Norwegian bachelor farmers (more à la Willa Cather than Garrison Keillor) who had signed up for the same program as Dad. The Haugens, when their spirits willed it, ate ice cream (Ole) right out of the carton in Baumann's grocery store, or beef stew (Herman) straight from the Dinty Moore can in his car, often parked in front of a bar on Main Street. Mom and Eleanore never used the word *indolent*, but if they had, their condemnation of the Haugens would have been gentler.

As I recall, Mom never made a distinction between Dad and the Haugens when she and Eleanore gossiped. I imagined Mom took it on faith that our situation was incomparable to that of the Haugens because Dad (who wasn't much of a drinker) continued to farm a quarter section of land, drove a school bus, and raised Suffolk sheep and a few Hereford cattle.

I began thinking differently, however, and not only because of Eleanore's comment about my dirty face. I was considering my other experiences with gossip. For instance, through accompanying Dad to the café or the barbershop, I already had listened to other farmers, a few businessmen (who evidently weren't concerned about offending customers), and wage-earning laborers add to the complaints and confabulations about a local land hog. I heard opinions about what the cause of the fire really was that razed a barn the land hog and his brothers owned. About how the center of a barley field actually contained wheat so that the land hog could exceed his government-allotted wheat acreage base. About how no one present at these discussions would ever sign a contract with the land hog without first having read the fine print with a microscope.

One time, the land hog was present when the subject of coffee shop chatter turned to the five steel bins going up on our farm. Based on stipulations of the government program financing the construction, we ended up with four bins stretching more than thirty feet tall and one bin squatting half that height. The conservative anti–New Deal conversationalists present were ribbing Dad about that short bin. To my surprise, the land hog, a conservative himself, came to Dad's defense. He said, "I don't know about any of you, but that bin would be tall enough for me if it were

filled with one hundred dollar bills." I went home thinking the land hog was not only crafty but clever, too. Maybe
even compassionate, in that misguided way that has misery loving its company.

Criticism can yield gossip, but what is the difference
between nasty criticism and camouflaged criticism? The
former is a seedling that can mature into a plant with only
the water of retelling. The latter, such as Eleanore's "dirty
face" comment or the critique of our grain bin's diminutive stature, requires another nutrient: familiarity. People
who ridicule face-to-face need to be certain of the reaction
they'll receive. This behavior requires relationships fertil-
ized with knowledge, those in which a condemned person's response is as predictable as his or her wave, laugh,
or walk. Largely immobile, close-knit communities provide
the ideal breeding ground for this type of imperfection.

Taken a step further, an awareness of mannerisms
allows for theatrical criticism, and as I know, mimicry can
be irresistible. During our many Sunday dinners at the
Gateway Hotel, I studied its proprietor, Howard Henry,
whose nervous energy kept him scurrying about the café,
visiting customers, most of whom were friends (generally
all were acquaintances), checking in with the cooks in
the kitchen, and appraising the buffet. A fat man, Henry
already was the butt of much invective, but when I saw
him one Sunday snatch a deviled egg from a plate on the
buffet line and swallow it in one bite without breaking
stride as he hurried by, I recognized the gossipy move-
ments for a mime. I performed my nasty routine only
before special audiences because Henry was Dad's friend.
And because I was the breeder of this noxious weed, it
was tinted with hypocrisy's hue: I, too, was fat at the time

and had experienced abuses similar to the ones directed at Henry. Also, I could easily recall how red Mom's face had turned the Sunday she realized the land hog was seated at a café table next to ours (on Mom's blind side) and had heard all she'd said about him.

Having been both a victim and a perpetrator of gossip, I was intrigued as an adult by the idea that there can be positive, healing aspects to gossip. Kathleen Norris, author of *Dakota: A Spiritual Geography,* proposes such in an essay titled "The Holy Use of Gossip." Norris believes the vastness of the Great Plains, with its unrelenting climate and economic perils, impels us to allow our "human activity" to become "public property" so as to convince ourselves that we are part of a "caring community." Norris says, "Allowing yourself to be a subject of gossip is one of the sacrifices you make, living in a small town." A sacrifice, of course, only when the gossip originates from criticism because earlier in her essay Norris proclaims that "gossip done well can be a holy thing. It can strengthen communal bonds."

While gossip may abound in small-town America, it certainly can flourish in cities and suburbs as well. In fact, I first began thinking of an interesting aspect of gossip while working at North Dakota's land grant university. A coworker habitually began stories about her husband by saying "poor Milt." This tic prompted others to wonder aloud whether Milt might be her husband's middle name. I've since thought it logical to mimic my friend's unintended tactic—that is, to take the initiative with respect to gossip, so as to provide the fecundity it requires to meet Norris's criterion of being "done well."

And so, here is an anecdote I hope emits a carnation's perfume: In 2001, I attended the funeral of a man who had been one of Dad's best friends, "Young Bill" Ruelle, an octogenarian at death but nonetheless the son of Bill Ruelle the elder. From an earlier telephone conversation, I knew that Eleanore was accompanying Mom to Young Bill's funeral. I hadn't seen much of Eleanore since she'd had a stroke that affected her balance, and initially, I felt uncomfortable being around her at the funeral because I reflexively lunged for her every time she began wobbling.

With her cane centered directly in front of her, Eleanore swooped and swirled as if she were a top losing its momentum, almost as if she had complete control of her physical faculties but had the irresistible urge to break out into a dance routine to a tune such as "Puttin' on the Ritz." She always self-corrected, though, and by the time the funeral had concluded, I'd become familiar, and thus more comfortable, with Eleanore's involuntary gyrations.

After Young Bill's funeral, I drove Mom and Eleanore over to a fruit stand housed underneath a large tent on the south side of Minot. They'd seen an ad for Washington State peaches and wanted to buy some for canning. Even though it was early September, the temperature by noon was well into the eighties, and climbing, and so I drove right up to the tent entrance to drop them off.

By the time I'd parked the car and entered the tent, Mom and Eleanore were already halfway down one aisle. Two old ladies in their mideighties, both relying on canes, Mom waddling and Eleanore bebopping. Both squeezing and sniffing and finally selecting. As I watched Mom and Eleanore, I was reminded of older homes and antique wood furniture. Like the women's many physical infirmities, every creak or groan of a floorboard or crossbeam and every scratch or ding on an armrest or a rocker has a story to tell.

Once the old friends were back inside the air-conditioned comfort of Mom's car with their fruit squarely positioned on the backseat next to Eleanore, she said, "I'm not used to this royal treatment." My only response was to look at Eleanore in the rearview mirror and beam.

Eleanore's praise represents another source of gossip, the exaggerated claim, meant to honor the person to whom it refers—but a claim also running the risk of minimizing, by implication, the efforts of others. And so, while I was thankful for the news that Eleanore thought I'd turned out to be a good boy after all, I empathized with her daughter Jan, who married a local farmer and therefore had remained in the community, and who, I knew from conversations with Mom, was Eleanore's "faithful servant."

In her essay on gossip, Norris also says, "We are interrelated in a small town, whether or not we're related by blood." From this statement I infer that people often become friends in small towns because of circumstance more so than choice. Perhaps, but friends nevertheless. Mom and Eleanore had been K–12 schoolmates and, according to Mom, good friends all the while. Both had married hometown men and then became grounded in their community—that is, neither traveled outside North Dakota much, for many reasons, I suppose: lack of money or leisure time or desire.

Most, if not all, of Mom's out-of-state adventures included Dad and resulted from their involvement with the North Dakota Farmers Union. Suffice to say, Mom and Dad's mismatched 1950s-vintage Samsonite suitcases, which Mom stored underneath their bed, didn't get much use, at least in the conventional sense. The suitcase with a herringbone tweed pattern, however, saw constant use because it was where Mom stored most of the Avon products she bought, on faith, from Eleanore, who, based on appearance, didn't use any more of what she sold than Mom used of what she bought.

Nonetheless, this exchange helped Mom fill a need. With a suitcase crammed full of perfumes, soaps, powders, and whatever else Eleanore had recommended, with the center drawer of our kidney-shaped cherry wood writing desk overflowing with greeting cards for all occasions, and with our freezer, plus several canisters tucked away in various kitchen cabinets, holding a ready reserve of baked goods, Mom was perpetually prepared for any unexpected event, good or bad. Mom's Avon suitcase remained chock-full for as long as I lived at home.

After Mom and Dad had retired and he had died, I would call Mom many, many times, only to hear a busy signal that might echo across two hours. Once I got through and asked Mom who she'd been talking to (although I had a pretty good idea), Mom's reply typically went something like this: "Oh, that darned Eleanore. You just can't get rid of her." One question I never asked Mom was this: how many times was it you who called her?

After Mom was hospitalized and subsequently diagnosed with inoperable ovarian cancer, I spent many nights sleeping on the couch in her home. My routine was to get to Westhope from the hospital in Minot by nine o'clock at night and then head out for the hospital by midmorning. During the first week of Mom's hospitalization, she had been alert enough and in good enough spirits to talk with friends on the phone, including Eleanore. Even so, the first night I slept at Mom's, her phone rang, and I heard: "Dean, this is Eleanore. How is Vivian?"

These evening conversations between Eleanore and me, each beginning with "Dean, this is Eleanore," continued until the night Mom died. When Eleanore called that night, I struggled to steady my voice, the effort of which made my throat throb and ache. I told Eleanore only that Mom had had a tough day. Minutes after Eleanore and I had hung up, Mom's nurse called and told me she had died.

I didn't call Eleanore with the news until the next morning. From Eleanore I heard a slow leaking of air, forming the word "Ohhhh," reverberating with the stoic, resigned tone I'd heard all my small-town life.

Mom was especially dismayed that she got sick in the spring because she would not be able to enjoy the routine of buying and planting her annual flowers. After she found out that the rest of her life would—best-case scenario—involve a nursing home, she sporadically launched into narratives about her perennial flowers, all of which she had marked off with orange plastic flags attached to wire stakes so that spring tillage damaged none.

"You and Nicki take my daisies," Mom said. "What else do you want?"

"Don't worry about it, Mom. We've got enough flowers."

"Have Joann Henry come over and dig up some of my bleeding heart. She's a real flower gal. I've got some glad bulbs ordered. Give those to Joann, too. And my irises must be about ready to bloom. Eleanore gave those to me. She should have them."

"Shouldn't you transplant irises in the fall?" I asked.

"It'll be OK."

In the spring Westhope has a citywide rummage sale, which in 2003 coincided closely with Mom's death and the sale of her home. One Friday afternoon as Nicki and I were preparing for the sale by arranging stacks on tables in the garage, Eleanore parked her midsized Ford (a better fit for her) in the cul-de-sac and then bobbed and weaved up the slanting driveway. We talked about the weather, the progress of spring planting, hers and the farmers', and all the while, it felt good having one of Mom's friends nearby. After only a few minutes, Eleanore danced back to her car and left.

When we were arranging Mom's suitcases for sale, I didn't sniff, but I imagine the scent of Avon products probably still lingered inside one. Chuck Armer bought the suitcases. Chuck, the sixty-something handyman who had mowed Mom's lawn and provided her with a variety of other services, such as putting up and taking down her Christmas lights and weeding her garden. Mom said Chuck had been a smart high school student. He worked on road construction for a while, but after witnessing a worker get crushed, Chuck quit his job and lived with his parents until they died. Afterward, he became the lone human occupant of the family home, shared with many cats (a knowledgeable Westhope-ite put the total at more than twenty).

Like Mom, Eleanore relied on Chuck for lawn mowing and other odd jobs, and Mom told me many times that Eleanore and she were the only women in town to feed Chuck dinner or supper when he happened to be working for them around mealtime. Mom's addendum: "Eleanore and I always say that if he's good enough to work for us, he's good enough to eat with us." I've never heard an argument against this vision of social justice I could accept.

Mostly because of his financial circumstances, I suspect, Chuck has traveled infrequently—for example, an occasional trip to Montana to visit his younger brother Larry. And yet, Chuck's comment upon buying Mom's suitcases was, "Oh, these will come in handy," which also is what he said about Mom's toaster oven, her TV, and the twenty or so one-gallon water jugs I gave him.

As we were readying for the rummage sale, Nicki and I were also assuming the role of cemetery caretaker for the graves of Mom, Dad, my two older siblings who died as infants, and those of my Hulse grandparents and great-grandparents. When we were buying silk arrangements at the local floral shop, its owner told us a story: Eleanore had been in the previous week to buy bedding plants. As she was paying for her flowers, Eleanore had commented about how she and Mom had been talking about the work they faced come planting season. Eleanore concluded, "Vivian got out of it." This gossip, done well, shared by an unrelated-yet-interrelated member of a small-town community, soothed like the scent of lilac.

After we sold and closed on Mom's house, my only links to my hometown that summer were the local newspaper, an occasional call to Mom's sister Ruth, and my one-day jaunt, in mid-August, for the flower show, part of which involved a tribute to Mom for her many years of membership in the Westhope Garden Club. There were so many people who wanted to visit that day, Eleanore among them.

A few weeks later I was stunned to see Eleanore's picture accompanying her obituary in a September issue of the *Westhope Standard*. Coincidentally, Nicki and I had been planning a trip to Westhope to remove the silk flowers from graves the following weekend. Once there, we talked to Chuck, who sadly and respectfully repeated the last conversation he'd had with Eleanore. Later, we saw Eleanore's daughters, Carol, who moved to Minnesota after high school, and farmer-daughter Jan. They were taking a lunch break at the local café, and we offered our condolences.

Jan said, "Mom sure missed Vivian."

Simon and Garfunkel first released a song titled "Old Friends," which includes the lyric "How terribly strange to be seventy," when I was young enough to be hurt by Eleanore's backhanded compliment about my dirty face. In 1996, chance played this song for me as I was en route to a wedding, in which I was to be the middle-aged best man. This friend, my best man twenty years earlier, moved to my hometown in 1969, and our friendship began assuming its character amid a troupe of rebellious teens acting out on a small-town stage. Since then, we have never managed to live near one another for more than a few months at a time. In fact, circumstances have had him living mostly in major metropolitan areas many states away.

As I drove along the freeway that day in 1996 listening to chance's selection, I shuddered at the thought of our growing old. Now when I consider the terrible strangeness of friends descending into the valley of their seventies, I have the image of Mom and Eleanore, old, old friends, walking together, gracefully, amid the shadows of their eighties. And, intertwined with this image is my conviction that gossip done well can cause flowers to bloom where the sun doesn't shine.

It Takes an Appetite

Because my wife and I chose not to have children, I have no experience in determining whether it really takes a village to raise a child. My childhood memories, however, remind me that rituals involving handmade food are acts of communion.

On the stovetop, Mom's gray fudge pan, its black handle worn to the blond wood in many places. From where I stand, I see only steam rising, like a pavement mirage on a scorching summer day. I know from the aroma that its contents are an evolving concoction of sugar, cream, and unsweetened chocolate squares that must melt and bubble to the soft ball stage on a candy thermometer. Once the pan becomes cool enough for Mom to handle, she cradles it in the crook of her left arm. Gripping her trusty spoon with her right hand, she stirs and stirs and stirs, and her breaths, becoming louder, match up with her arm motion. She incorporates air into this chocolaty mass until it is a few shades lighter than a Tootsie Roll and achieves a creaminess that butter would envy. After she's coaxed the candy into a dish, where it will set up for cutting, Mom lets me scrape away what little fudge clings to the inside of the pan. Each time, I enjoy these velvety remnants as if I've never had this sweet treat before. Later, Dad and I will get to eat the few pieces that Mom deems too imperfect to offer friends and neighbors. She shares her fudge winter, spring, summer, and fall.

All those containers of confectioneries were gestures
of love substituting for words, tougher to raise than roses
for Mom and many like her. During the holiday season,
Mom's fudge became the centerpiece of her gift platters,
which she arranged as artfully as the prize-winning bouquets she entered in flower shows. Other elements of
her edible art included penuche (brown sugar fudge, my
favorite), divinity (as airy as I imagine a cloud to be and
as sweet tasting as forgiveness), powdered-sugary Mexi-
can wedding cookies, toffee adorned with chocolate shav-
ings and chopped walnuts, and other hard candies, the
most memorable of which were red and green, licorice
flavored.

For Mom's chocolate-covered specialties, such as peanut butter logs, coconut balls, and cherries, she enlisted a
double boiler, sheets of waxed paper, and many round
toothpicks. After manipulating the peanut butter and coconut conglomerations and after drying the maraschino cherries and wrapping each in sugar-and-corn-syrup dough,
Mom aligned the ovals and orbs in orderly rows on waxed
paper. She then skewered each piece with a toothpick,
swirled it through a bath of melted confectioners' chocolate, and then eased it back onto the waxed paper. She
removed the toothpicks with other toothpicks—that is, by
pushing against the candy with a free pick precisely at the
other pick's insertion point and simultaneously pulling it
out. Her final act of orderliness was to dip the tip of a pick
into the melted chocolate and "paint" over the hole the
formerly inserted pick had occupied. Laborious, meticulous, hours long, this process continued each and every
year from my birth (and before) until Mom's death. The
literal last pieces of those candies, remaining in Mom's

freezer when we cleared out her house, I viewed with King Midas's eyes.

When I was a child, Dad and I spent many hours stretching across many days making holiday deliveries to family and friends in town and in the country. Many of these friends reciprocated by having us in for coffee or by sending us home with a bundle of their own homemade treats. Even though Mom and Dad frequently discussed our finances during supper, and often asked my thoughts about a particular spending decision, they never fretted about how much of our money went into the goodies they made and gave away.

One holiday visit that sticks in my memory involves "Pepper" Martin, the town's grave digger. Pepper lived, literally, in a tar paper shack, and he died so long ago that I've forgotten his real name, if I ever knew it.

"Why are we going to see him?" I asked.

"Because he's alone, and it's Christmas," Dad said.

Pepper drove a pickup truck that was quite similar to ours, except I had judged it to be in better condition than ours. And so, I once had posed a question to Dad pertaining to why we couldn't afford a truck better than the grave digger's. My answer was one of those looks from Dad that silently spoke: "You know better than to be envious."

On the day we called on Pepper, it was North Dakota cold. I studied how Pepper had banked snow, several feet high, all around the outside of his house, which couldn't have been much larger than ten feet by twenty feet (it was razed immediately after Pepper died in the 1960s). Dad knocked and within seconds it was a startled Pepper who opened the door. Eyes wide open and unshaven, as he usually was, Pepper smiled as soon as he fixed his gaze on the gaily wrapped box in Dad's hands. Pepper's gap-toothed grin, likewise, familiar. Wearing woolen long underwear, the top portion of which was serving as his shirt, Pepper invited us in. Pepper's home was warm, clean, tidy, and small: a main room and a bedroom, and perhaps a bathroom. Perhaps. Near the center of the main room was Pepper's heat source, a coal furnace with a cooking surface on top, its dented, patched-up chimney meandering up and out through the roof. Something was bubbling in a saucepan on the cooktop, and it smelled good. Dad offered Pepper the gift, which he accepted with many, many thanks, and that was the extent of our stay.

Except. A few months afterward, our minister drew his sermon from the Gospel according to Matthew, and when he repeated the following words, my mind's eye saw Pepper Martin's face: "Inasmuch as ye have done it unto one of the least of these, My brethren, ye have done it unto Me." I can picture Pepper Martin's face still.

After Mom died, a K–12 classmate of mine, Darlene Cameron (née Rauk), asked for Mom's fudge recipe. The request came embedded in an e-mail from her husband, Don (whom I still like to call "Hoot," the childhood nickname his dad gave him). Mom had told me that Darlene became an exceptional baker ("lovely buns") after marrying Hoot. Mom attributed Darlene's skill to her mom, Marie. And so, I was glad that a good cook wanted to carry on Mom's tradition. I sent the recipe, along with a warning about using an inaccurate thermometer, as I recently had done, and the hockey-puck hardness of overboiled fudge.

Our Christmas card from the Camerons that year included a thank-you note from Darlene. Besides reporting on her success with candy making, Darlene recounted how their winter had been going, how their neighbor, Myron Lodoen, had been feeding some of the hay he put up for his cattle to all the deer that were congregating around their neighboring farmsteads.

Of course, Darlene didn't write "Myron Lodoen"; she wrote only "Myron." His parents, Hazel and "Wood" (a nickname reflecting his baseball prowess as a young man), had been annual recipients of Mom's Christmas goodies. When Dad and I made deliveries to the Lodoens, Hazel treated me to oatmeal-raisin cookies and wide strips of chocolate licorice, which she kept in decorative jars on her kitchen counter. Hazel always sent Dad and me home with a holiday package, too.

As I read Darlene's note, I could see stubble fields, the prairie road dividing the Cameron and Lodoen farmsteads along a section boundary, the trees where I imagined the deer to be feasting. I saw all this through the mind's eye of someone who had moved away a quarter century earlier. The scenes Darlene's words painted for me were as comforting as memories of Mom's fudge and Hazel's cookies.

"I sure miss your dad's sour cream raisin pies." This from Jim Artz, an overweight middle-aged man one year my senior, a son of Dad's best friend during his retirement years. Dad and Harold Artz's friendship was forged by a mutual love of farming, horses, and food. Jim's lament, offered with a weak smile, came in a conversation during my hometown's centennial celebration.

Harold had died less than a year earlier, eleven years after Dad had died and only a few months after Mom died.

Dad often teased Mom about Harold because in their youth Mom supposedly had loaned Harold one of her shoulders to cry on at a dance the night Harold's girl broke up with him—the girl he believed to be the love of his life. Mom and Harold never dated, and Harold eventually wed Jean, who became the mother of fifteen Artz children.

Mom told me that Jim and Harold had feuded after Harold retired from farming. I'm familiar with family feuds. Jim's smile lingered after he mentioned Dad's pies, as if he were still thinking of sweet bygone days. Already, I had begun tasting his hunger.

It was only after Mom died and I had inherited the family photo albums that I noticed she had dutifully archived nearly twenty similar images: people posing with angel food cakes, all Dad's creations. Dad once was disqualified from a cake-baking contest at the state fair in Minot because the judges concluded he was a professional. Dad's cakes truly were that good.

Dad's secret was his technique. First, he sifted the cake flour four times. The sifter's rhythm was steady but sing-songy. Afterward, Dad gently folded the flour, one-fourth of it at a time, into his beaten egg whites, which formed peaks that were neither too soft nor too stiff. Just right. Dad used a wire whip for folding the flour into the egg whites and a bottom-up motion that caused the utensil to contact the glass mixing bowl and say *whip, whip, whip.* When ready for the cake pan, Dad's batter was perfumed with the extracted aromas of vanilla and coconut and almonds and was as airy and as glossy as raw meringue. Fresh-fallen snow that the wind has sculpted into drifts reminds me of Dad's dollopy cake batter. And I can easily conjure an image of one of Dad's just-baked cakes, cooling, its three-pronged round pan inverted, each prong positioned on an enameled coffee cup, chipped from use, keeping the delicacy as light as its name implies. Dad's best guess was that he made about fifteen hundred such cakes, the majority of which he made from memory without relying on a recipe.

Missing from Mom's photos of people with Dad's cakes is the image of I. B. Olson, Westhope's former fix-it man. As with Pepper Martin, I can't remember what I. B.'s name was (he, of course, is dead now, too). Once those of my generation became teenagers, we shortened his name to one syllable: "Ib."

Dad annually took our swather canvas to I. B. so that he could patch a new piece over a hole, mend a tear, or replace some laths. And it is upon the repair of sundry components of farm machinery that my memory of I. B.'s shop hangs. I smell oily canvas, hear the clatter of an industrial sewing machine, and see sunshine, laden with airborne dust particles, streaming from south-facing windows. Light, feeding I. B.'s potted plants, red-flowering geraniums mostly. I see his workbench, which occupies the center of his shop, and on its surface sit coffee cans nearly overflowing with bolts of various sizes and glass jars full of cotter pins and rivets. Elsewhere, all types of smallish hammers for delicate tapping. A vise. Odd-sized scraps of metal. Copper pipe and other assorted supplies for his son's plumbing business likewise lying hither or hithermost. This scene was as familiar as I. B. himself: wire-rimmed glasses hanging on the end of his nose, combed-back hair (varying shades of gray throughout my life), similar gray work shirt and pants, arms and legs disproportionate to his compact torso, a protruding belly, long, slender fingers, somewhat misshaped by age, with equally long, dirty fingernails, perhaps for plucking items such as tiny nails or tacks from storage containers.

I. B. could fix anything that didn't involve electrical wiring, and so it was that Dad began taking kitchen gadgets to him. First our pancake griddle, suffering from a broken plastic leg. I. B. refitted the griddle with hand-fabricated metal legs he painted black. This retrofit lasted Mom and Dad the rest of their lives. One of the last items Dad took to I. B. for repair was his hand-cranked eggbeater, its black plastic handle broken. I. B. fashioned a wooden grip and painted it bright blue. Likewise, this repair served Dad for all the cakes he had left to bake.

I. B. didn't charge Dad for fixing his eggbeater, so to show his gratitude, Dad baked I. B. a cake. I imagine they joked about who got the better end of that deal, but not having been present for their discussion, I can't say what conclusion they reached. I can speculate, however, that a cliché used to the extreme in weekly small-town newspapers applied to their exchange: "A good time was had by all."

A Witness on the
Home Front

Our picnic lunch included crusty hearth-baked bread, a tortellini salad, and for dessert, flaky, date-filled rugalach—all from a neighborhood delicatessen. Nicki and I thought we should splurge on the outdoor eats because we were saving money by staying with a friend, and because I was only weeks into my forties. Another birthday party. We ate our meal on the Capitol lawn as we listened (along with thousands upon thousands of others) to the National Symphony Orchestra. We visited museums and art galleries, too, during our stay in Washington, D.C. At the Phillips, Renoir's *The Luncheon of the Boating Party* spoke to me from two rooms away.

While running along Sixteenth Street, still several blocks from the White House, I saw other sights: decrepit buildings, oases of stench and shattered glass, and a drunken white man, sitting on a short wall in front of a decaying house. He was pivoting to and fro, side to side, like a joystick, hollering himself hoarse at 8:30 a.m. I turned back before I reached the White House after I saw a black man standing near a bus stop. Bandaged with the gauzy wrappings of an emergency room, his head wounds still seeped blood.

For me those contrasting scenes of culture and crisis symbolize a struggle that pits freedom of choice and justice against progress hitched only to profits. Nearly all my life I've seen this battle rage as a bloodless coup in North Dakota. Only in recent years have I begun wondering whether I have spent most of my adult life living on North Dakota's largest reservation. How so? For decades, the word describing North Dakota's population has been *out-migration.* While several cities, Fargo included, enjoy growth, the countryside has been depopulating, and the net effect has been a state in relative stasis. This circumstance raises a question: are growth and development synonymous? My answer: it depends upon whom you ask.

Having been born in 1955 and having grown up on a family farm, I can bear witness to former U.S. Secretary of Agriculture Earl Butz's infamous advice to farmers. Butz told farmers to till and plant everything except the fencerows. I observed the fate of a so-called progressive farmer from Westhope who heeded the Butz gospel. In the mid-1970s, Ernie Sivertson rented some of our farm. He plowed up land that had been in pasture for decades. Ernie removed mile after mile of fence, that which was still usable and that which was not. Ernie's attempt to turn our farm into a factory was exemplary. He was one of the first farmers in the area to diversify into sunflowers. And yet, Ernie exited farming after the agricultural crisis of the 1980s shredded his paper equity, the key criterion for determining someone's fitness to farm as an industrialist.

Although Ernie's son, Harley, has managed to continue farming, the evisceration of North Dakota's countryside continues. For example, the U.S. Department of Agriculture reports that the state lost about twenty-five hundred farms in the 1990s. Only six of the state's fifty-three counties gained population during the 1990s. Cass

County, home to Fargo, gained the most, more than twenty thousand people. Census figures for 2000 showed that North Dakota has thirty-six counties (out of fifty-three) with population densities of fewer than six people per square mile.

Nicki and I were among those who helped swell Fargo's population during the decade of the 1970s. We quit farming after only two seasons, in 1979, before the ensuing calamity hit. However, we are neither soothsayers nor economic sophisticates. A key reason we got out of farming has roots in my agricultural philosophy: I oppose the view that a farm is a factory, which its "operator" can make maximally efficient through the constant accumulation of costly, complex machines, reliance on an increasing array of fossil fuel–derived chemicals, and most recently, the use of transgenic crop varieties containing genes from totally unrelated organisms.

For nearly three decades I've witnessed the changes occurring in Fargo as I've driven or run along the city's streets and avenues. When training for a marathon in 1999, I fashioned an eight-mile course so that it included a favorite avenue. Some unsettling progress has occurred along this route at an intersection where in 1979 there sat only the headquarters for Blue Cross Blue Shield of North Dakota, and directly to the north of it, a farmstead. I knew the elderly man and woman who lived on that farmstead—not by name, but by their outdoor activities.

That farmstead was aesthetically pleasing to me because of its two white barns, each of which had green trim and matching green shingles. Also on the property were two small houses and some fenced pasture. And as is the case with many North Dakota farmsteads, there were pieces of abandoned machinery rusting away in a shelter-belt north of the buildings. On the southeast edge of the farmstead, near a profusion of lilacs, sat a hayfield, only a few acres, which the old man cut and baled every June and, moisture permitting, once again in late July or early August. If I was fortunate enough to be running by the farmstead during haying season, my reward was free samples of a natural perfume, accompanied by flashbacks of friendship.

Before I was born, Dad and Albert Madsen, a neighbor and one of Dad's best friends, had begun sharing a hay baler, the type producing small, square bales weighing less than one hundred pounds. By the time I was old enough to tag along with Dad, that old International Harvester baler seemed to break down every day. Eventually, Dad and Albert were able to trade our old baler for a new one, but that old red "S.O.B." remained the subject of conversations between Dad and Albert as long as Albert lived.

My recollections of haying season are also full of sounds as well as smells. I can still hear the trilled curses that a breakdown produced. That chorus always played into a crescendo of laughter, followed by a diminuendo, and then deep sighs. I learned how to drive a tractor before I grew strong enough to hoist bales, and so I piloted the caravan of tractor, baler, and hayrack around and around the fields while Dad and either Albert or his son, Jon, toiled. Our procession was timed to the *pop-pop* beat of a two-cylinder John Deere engine, and I strained to hear as they chattered and cackled while sweating and plucking and then neatly stacking the bales on the rack. From my generation's perspective, no work on the farm was as physically demanding as baling hay, but because of our partnership with the Madsens, none was as emotionally satisfying either.

Years after Jon had moved to Indianapolis, he stopped by to see Dad during a trip home to visit his mother, Nell. He brought Dad a framed photograph of the old IH baler. Taped to the glass was a handmade label stating, "That S.O.B." To get the shot, Jon had to cross a barbed wire fence and then work his way down the side of a steep coulee to reach the spot where the baler's last owner literally had put it out to pasture. No doubt, stubborn weeds such as sow thistle and a host of prairie grasses were intent on consuming the baler where it sat rusting away. And so Jon most likely did some clearing before snapping his picture. Having become overweight at middle age as a result of well-ingrained eating habits and a "paper pusher" job in the insurance industry, Jon just might have sweated as much while taking that photo as he did while baling hay decades earlier when he was a svelte teenager.

Dad received Jon's photo in retirement, after he had lost a leg to diabetes. Although I wasn't present for Jon's visit, Dad's retelling of it convinced me that their laughter resonated with a familiarity time had failed to weather.

Like Jon and me, that Fargo farmstead became citified. In the 1990s, the rusting machinery got recycled, without question an improvement. The houses vanished. The shelterbelt disappeared, too, most likely returned to the dust and ashes from whence it came. But the barns saw "life" after relocation. The smaller barn is now a building component of a YMCA. The larger dairy barn, property of the Fargo Park District, now functions mainly as a storage facility.

I know I should be grateful to these nonprofit organizations for preserving such relics of the past, but there is a maddening irony present in this new setting: while both barns sit amid modern structures in a commercial development, it has become the fate of the dairy barn to have as one of its closest neighbors a building housing the Cargill Financial Service Center.

Cargill began as a privately owned buyer and reseller of grain, a wholesale function personified: middleman. Still privately owned, Cargill has expanded into other ventures and operates globally. All of Dad's life he believed Cargill was too big, had too few competitors bidding against it for his grain, a circumstance that he felt allowed Cargill to offer farmers less money for their grain than was fair. In Dad's view, one way to defend against such powerful corporations was to form member-owned cooperatives.

The supply cooperative Dad devoted much of his energy to was the Farmers Union, which became known as Cenex during Dad's lifetime. Dad served on the board of directors for his local co-op station for twenty-five years. His support was so intense that he would not buy gasoline from any other station—especially not a Standard or an Amoco station—even if it meant driving several miles to find a lonely Cenex store. When Nicki and I lived in West Fargo, Dad, retired then, thought nothing of driving the ten- or fifteen-mile round-trip from our rented condo through Fargo, across the Red River, and into Moorhead, Minnesota, so that he could fill up at the Cenex station there. When he still farmed, Dad patronized our local Cenex station with a fervor few could match. He purchased tires for cars, trucks, tractors, and implements. He bought oil and grease in bulk. He picked up batteries,

chains, nuts, bolts, wrenches, and other sundry farm supplies on an as-needed basis. Laundry soap, too, along with
a washer and dryer, a refrigerator, and a stove.

Dad was at once intense and easygoing. I sometimes
fear that my exercising and my dread of diabetes, based
on Dad's outcomes, have caused me to draw only upon
the intensity I inherited from him. I may be squandering a
finite resource because energy spent on selfish endeavors
provides no lessons on civic responsibility. I often think
about Dad and wonder how he could maintain for so long
his desire to fight what he thought was the good fight. The
only conclusion I can reach is that his experiences with
corporations such as Cargill so inflamed his sense of injus-
tice that he converted anger into determination, and what
George Orwell and others have tried to achieve through
their writing, Dad attempted through his activism.

After development of the Fargo farmstead, much of the
area became pavement—most of the hayfield, too. A sign
implies that the property will forever be called the Rabanus Center, in recognition of the people who lived there
And so land that once produced food and a small-scale
sense of responsibility became home to several national
franchises: among these, an office supply outlet, a toy
store, and a doughnut shop.

I bought a desk chair from that office supply chain.
The in-store promotion described the chair as being sleek
and functional. I suddenly felt like Voltaire's Pangloss, believing in the best of all possible worlds. My faith was
short lived, though. Included among the chair's packaging
and assembly instructions was a bright orange card containing the following message: "If you are experiencing
any problems with your chair, or are missing any parts,

please DO NOT RETURN TO STORE. Please call customer service at 1-800- . . ."

My computer desk came a few years earlier from what some might call a mom-and-pop operation, although the couple who owned the furniture store composed a pair of twenty-somethings. This business, too, was a franchise, offering mass-produced solid-wood furniture. The wife was generous with her time in helping me select a stain. Perhaps because of her enthusiasm for her work, she seemed to coo when agreeing with my choice: a light-reddish mahogany. Her husband did the staining himself, he attached a slide-out tray for my computer keyboard, he delivered my desk in the backseat of his car, and after he'd toted its components inside our home, he assembled it. But the couple's small business failed, and the space their hope once occupied was rented again by the time I was running past the site in 1999.

That same year I took my favorite "country run" when I visited Mom in Westhope. This rectangular route is bounded now on its northeast side by a sign reading "107th Street Northwest," a somewhat confusing 9-1-1 euphemism necessitated by rural depopulation that makes it easier for strangers to respond to the distress calls of other strangers. My run followed a flooding rainfall, and so I was serenaded by thousands of nesting ducks. Along the soggier portions of the course, ditches brimmed with cattails dancing in the breeze. Another treat: the sweet incense produced by a farmer burning dead grass, a rite of passage as familiar to me as the migration of waterfowl.

Near the midway point of that twelve-mile course, an approach juts northward into a field. I've always used this access point as a landmark to remind me where the Hulse School sat. The building disappeared years before I was born, but Dad never tired of pointing out the spot where the school bearing our family's surname once stood.

About a mile west of where the Hulse School stood, there remains a cow pasture, which contains a large wetland fed by what maps of a certain vintage prepared by the U.S. Geological Survey have dubbed the Hulse Coulee. That pasture and slough were part of the first family farm the Hulses owned in Bottineau County. As with the Hulse School, Dad eagerly and repeatedly pointed to the ponded summertime water and then proceeded to tell me about the skating rink and how farm kids came from miles around to skate.

"When we were kids, we used grain shovels for sleds," Dad told me once after a blizzard had sculpted a fifteen-foot-high snowbank in our barnyard. And so I spent much of one sunny, frigid afternoon sliding on an aluminum scoop, using its handle like a joystick.

During my adulthood, I've come to realize there are many perspectives about recreation. The "shop 'til you drop" ethic functions as the vanguard of our consumerism. During the weekend-long coronation of Harry Potter as film icon, I visited the Toys "R" Us store located at the Rabanus Center. Outside, I was welcomed by a banner: "Now Hiring." Inside, a smiling greeter handed me a sale catalog and thanked me for shopping.

I walked by the hanging stuffed animals, which I was surprised to see were more prominently positioned than were the Harry Potter toys. I wondered whether stuffed animals could be more profitable than other toys. I was several strides down an aisle of board games before I noticed how unnaturally blue the lighting seemed. A mood-altering effect? Perhaps, but probably not. Even I am not that cynical regarding the tactics of modern commerce. Next, I listened to children and their giggling and crying, manifestations of excitement and weariness. After eye-balling rows of bicycles and playpens, after sidestepping the line of kids waiting to play the latest computer game, after massaging a forty-dollar basketball to see whether it was made of real leather, I jerked to attention as an anony-mous voice emanating from the store's loudspeaker system commanded: "All cashiers to checkout, please. All cashiers to checkout." With the echo of that voice still reverberat-ing in my ears, I walked past the battery displays posi-tioned in front of and on top of several checkout counters and left the store. I was wondering whether we Americans are living in a service economy or a servant economy.

As I was driving away from the Rabanus Center that day, I noticed a feature of its parking lot. At the south end of the paved-over property, the pavement and curb opened onto a grassy area, the former hayfield. The curb opening allowed snow blade operators to push snow into the vacant lot. A good idea, probably, but my focus that day was not on the parking lot, but rather, on a dead spot close to where the pavement ended. I concluded that road salt may have caused the problem. That's too bad, because it was an abnormally warm late-fall day, and the grass was still green where it was growing. But not much was growing where I was looking.

A national doughnut franchise and its paved parking lot and drive-through lane took over the last bit of ground where fragrant, herbaceous hay was at once bountiful and beautiful. Because this franchise was the first of its kind in

North Dakota, the governor's wife came all the way from Bismarck to perform briefly, yet joyously, with a local dance team. The dancers appeared on local TV news—all the networks. They danced on the concrete-covered hayfield. Expectations were that the doughnuts would move forever forward along a conveyor. However, the franchise closed within a decade.

I take no joy from business failures, but I do struggle to find hope in what the tale of the temporary doughnuts may be implying. Could consumerism by way of a ubiquitous urban landscape be on the wane?

I'm cautiously optimistic about the increasing number of young people interested in alternative farming methods and concepts such as community-supported agriculture. More small farms and locally grown food. Many more farmers' markets. Personal relationships between food buyers and sellers. Am I envisioning the future? Perhaps, but I'm only cautiously optimistic because I recall an agricultural economist's presentation to wheat producers in the mid-1990s. The economist had graphically represented trend data to reflect demand for low-fat, carbohydrate-dense bread and pasta products. The chart promised limitless, inevitable growth. It wasn't a chronic naysayer who caused that economist's predictive sky to fall. It was Dr. Atkins and his diet.

If food is both life and lifestyle, why not make purchases with the same civic-mindedness as we cast our votes? If a more agrarian, small-scale agriculture offers hope for a depopulating countryside, why not support it? If enjoying locally produced foods in season helps reduce fossil fuel use and carbon dioxide emissions, aren't we having our fresh-baked cake and eating it, too?

The reshuffling of population I've experienced during my life has me believing that I might share a certain sense of loss, and hope, with a ghostly Assiniboine or Ojibwe hunter. As that hunter might have awaited the return of the bison more than a century ago, I, too, anticipate a day when we determine that cattle should no longer claim sole occupancy of many tracts along the Hulse Coulee near Westhope, where children were once plentiful and play-time was something kids concocted.

A Genetic Propensity
for Populism

In 1962 a brand-new Ford Galaxie 500, a burnt peanut and cream two-tone, became part of the scenery on the street running along the north side of the barbershop in Westhope. The car's owner, a bar manager at a joint a few doors south from the barbershop, parked it there with a frequency that implied a reserved space. When rainstorms halted farm chores, Dad and I loafed at the barbershop. I inhaled, and savored, Barbasol- and Brylcreem-type aromas from my post in one of the salmon-colored hard plastic chairs. I listened to adult conversations seeming to follow the *clip-clip* rhythm of a well-practiced scissor hand, and eventually, I gazed out a picture window, sometimes still rain streaked, at that Ford. The car's styling was somewhat boxy, and yet, I saw in its large bull's-eye taillights a hopeful, futuristic flair.

What my mind couldn't conceive in the summer of 1962 was the target that rural America had become. My experiences since then have underscored the graciousness of history, not because we can use it to foreshadow pitfalls, but rather for its gift of illuminating pathways leading out of such traps.

What kinds of traps? Picture this: instead of offering a puritanical visage similar to that represented by Grant Wood's *American Gothic,* a painter now might capture the essence of rural America by depicting a different belief system, one not embodied by the relative handful of citizens remaining in the countryside but rather by corporate directors in their boardrooms.

Economic policies are largely responsible for creating America's rural white space, an aspect that angers me, and yet, one perhaps even inconceivable to those composing in 1962 the Research and Policy Committee of the Committee for Economic Development (CED), which published in July of that year a booklet titled *An Adaptive Program for Agriculture.* Demonstrating dramatic irony as well as any thespian, the CED claimed that it was "enabling businessmen to demonstrate constructively their concern for the general welfare." The CED stressed that this demonstration of concern was "essential to the successful functioning of the free enterprise capitalist system."

A benevolent corporation? A quaint idea, that, to someone like Dad, a prairie populist who in 1962 still could recollect economic and social injustices from the 1920s and early 1930s as quickly as I could conjure mental facsimiles of Seattle's spanking new Space Needle. For most of my life, I put little stock in Dad's rants about a Westhope banker, Joe Page, whom I never knew but whom Dad and every other Hulse I ever asked blamed for a 1924 foreclosure. Sour grapes, I always thought, until I came across a tattered, paint-spattered copy of a book I never knew existed. I didn't find the book until after Dad and Mom had both died, and Nicki and I were clearing out Mom's house in 2003. That book, a biography of residents living in Crawford County, Illinois, in the early 1900s, offers a glimpse of the promises life held for the Hulse family before their move to North Dakota:

Farming as an occupation is engaging the time and attention of men of superior attainments, for they realize that never before has the science of farming been so developed. Lafayette Hulse, a farmer and stockraiser of Section 18, Oblong Township, Crawford County, Ill., is a man who has made farming pay, and although a young man has achieved success. . . . In 1907 oil was discovered on the home place, and there are now nineteen wells in active operation. Samuel Hulse, brother of Lafayette . . . is operating the old home in conjunction with Lafayette. . . . Both the Hulse brothers are Republicans and they are enterprising, progressive farmers and successful young business men, who enjoy in the highest degree the confidence and respect of their neighbors.

Sam Hulse was my grandfather, and his father, Oscar Monroe ("O. M."), moved the Hulses in 1909 from their Illinois farm of about 250 acres near Oblong to a North Dakota farm with a brick house, only a few years old, northwest of Westhope.

A widower who'd married a widow, O. M. had been serving as a county road commissioner in Illinois when he made the move and had "operated a threshing machine and sawmill for thirty-two years, and [was] one of the most enterprising men of his community." With the benefit of hindsight, I have questioned why O. M. simply didn't start another business in Oblong rather than risk the trek to North Dakota. I've since settled on the fact that he must have loved farming more than business. And, I'm sure all that oil money boosted his confidence, which may have helped convince him to ship farm machinery and somewhere between thirty and forty horses from Illinois to the Hulses' new North Dakota home, a farm containing about twelve hundred acres, enough land for O. M.'s twenty children and stepchildren.

In fact, an anecdote offered to me by an older cousin about his father, Jim, another of O. M.'s sons, gives me an idea of how the prospects of oil riches affect Hulse men. After oil had been discovered near Westhope in the early 1950s—within a few miles of land several Hulses owned—their expectations ran high. While fantasizing about oil money that never came his way, Jim said, "I'm going to buy me a car so big, I'll have to back it out of town."

O. M. had been born and raised in Ohio and then followed his father, Andrew Jackson "Jack" Hulse, to Indiana, and from there, to Illinois. I'm intrigued by why my great-great-great-grandparents named a son after a U.S. president, even if "Old Hickory" did hold office at the time of Jack's birth. My curiosity forms around the facts that Jack was "a lifelong Republican" and that our seventh president is linked with the formation of today's Democratic Party. But then, other portions of family history have worked to convince me that even five generations ago, Hulses favored populists more than they did party affiliation—and especially a populist like Jackson, who was responsible for killing the Second Bank of the United States, viewed by many at the time as being, according to the National Archives, a "greedy monopoly dominated by the rich American and foreign interests."

During my first visit to Oblong in the mid-1990s, I discovered it is home to the Illinois Oilfield Museum. My second visit to Oblong came five years later and was preceded by a stop at the Crawford County Courthouse in Robinson. With directions from clerks in the recorder's office, I was able to drive to our old home, and I discovered that the section containing much of the former Hulse land still had five producing oil wells. Several oil-storage tanks were sitting on land my family once owned.

No photos of Jack Hulse exist as far as I know. I have a hand-me-down snapshot of when the Hulses arrived in North Dakota, and it includes an unidentified O. M. The man I like to believe is my great-grandfather wears a bowler and sports a dark cookie-duster mustache. In this photo he's positioned near the center of about twenty-five people, including other men of varying ages also wearing ties and coats, a woman and young girl, both adorned with hats (standing next to O. M.), and even a black railroad porter in a crisp white jacket. The man I've convinced myself is O. M. is the only one in the photo holding a hand outward, slightly cupped, a position suggesting that he might be inspecting the North Dakota soil on which he stands.

I've tried to piece together some of the Hulse family's misfortunes from various legal instruments involving the exchange of farmland and have cobbled this chronology: a warranty deed, dated March 24, 1913, involving O. M. and the First National Bank of Westhope, with J. L. Page signing as the bank's liquidating agent; a contract for deed between O. M. and his children in May 1914, a cancella tion of the contract for deed between O. M. and his children in December 1915; and finally, the sheriff's deed in 1924, the year O. M. lost everything and died. Because I'm not a lawyer, I can't say whether any of those documents reveal improprieties (including the contract for deed for the Illinois land, which makes "all oil rights subject to an assignment to J. L. Page and the said parties of the second part"). It doesn't require legal training, though, to wonder why nineteen oils wells—some of which continued pumping for decades—could *not* have provided enough cash flow to weather any economic storm. What I know for a fact is that neither Grandpa Sam nor Dad was a Republican by the time I was born. Both were active members of the North Dakota Nonpartisan League (NPL), a political party composed of prairie populists.

The NPL is most famous (or infamous, depending upon one's perspective) for creating the nation's only state-owned mill and elevator and state-owned bank. These institutions served to wrest market power away from corporations, and each still operates today. A merger created the Democratic-NPL party a year after I was born, and Dad soon began his decadelong stint as a district chairman. When Dad died, I made sure that the left lapel of his suit coat displayed a small, gold-plated donkey, the symbol of the national Democratic Party. In other words, Dad took his political activism with him to the grave, and his fellow Democrats, who crowded the church for the funeral, thought my gesture fitting. The only tradition missing from Dad's funeral was his own often-repeated assessment of death: "Well, we lost another good Democrat."

A North Dakota historian dubbed the state's early development the "Too-Much Mistake," the physical evidence of which being too much infrastructure and too few people. Today, I wonder whether there can't also be too much *downsizing* and *outsourcing*. Can't there come a point beyond which efficiency yields only diminishing returns? Or put another way: Can't there be too few farms? Listen to Wendell Berry's wisdom echo in his phrase "monomania of bigness," from *The Unsettling of America*. Then ask, how many farms are enough anyhow? One per township? One per county? One per state? One?

The economic efficiency that persists in reducing the number of family farms has its roots in technology, and granted, it is responsible for an astonishing proliferation in farm productivity yielding more food choices for consumers and, I believe, undervalued food. This technology also carries with it too much—namely, a slew of complex environmental problems ranging from soil erosion to water pollution to the loss of plant and animal species to direct threats to human health. Addressing these types of problems did not become ingrained in U.S. policy until 1970 with the creation of the Environmental Protection Agency, whose existence many credit to Rachel Carson's *Silent Spring,* first published in 1962, in which the author writes about chemicals such as Monsanto's DDT, now banned in the United States.

Like Jack, O. M., Grandpa Sam, and Dad, I have watched "the science of farming" develop. During my lifetime, it has pushed the concept of reductionism to levels that threaten the diversity of life itself. Furthermore, it has spawned so-called substantial equivalents, which are not scientific triumphs of discovery derived from biotechnology but rather products of the political process. Analyses of molecular components, no matter how mystifyingly cutting edge, cannot transform three hundred copper pennies into a piece of paper currency worth three dollars without some sleight of hand.

And so my good fight is for the survival of small farms and rural communities. Among the modelers of a postindustrial strategy are, ironically and fittingly, the many American Indian tribes working to reclaim their lands and their cultures. I am thrilled by the prospect of comparatively small bison herds once again roaming and sustaining the Northern Plains. I am hopeful that this time around all who wish to reside on the Great Plains can work together to achieve their goals. Why not expect disparate people and cultures to flourish amid a diverse landscape? I, too, am excited by the ideas of scientist-philosophers such as Wes Jackson and Allan Savory, who offer holistic approaches that appreciate the abundance of plant and animal species and encourage farmers and ranchers to work in harmony with nature and thereby reduce their costs of production, stemming in large part from their present reliance on synthetic solutions supplied by middlemen.

In many ways I see my purpose dovetailing with what has passed. I believe that Dad's rage against the dark economic forces he faced was akin to what moved my great-great-great-grandparents 130 years earlier to name their son Andrew Jackson.

Directed by the CED's bylaws calling for "the attainment and maintenance of high and secure standards of living for people in all walks of life," the committee identified in 1962 several obstacles for agriculture. Committee members concluded, "What we have in mind in our program is a reduction of the farm labor force on the order of one third in a period of not more than five years." In newer eras, politicians alluded to the CED's adaptive approach by calling it compassionate conservatism, a kinder, gentler laissez-faire model, one that, as the committee stressed, "seeks to achieve adjustment to economic reality without imposing hardships." These statements stand as oversimplifications or outright deceptions.

The events of recent history make clear to me that the type of economic reality the CED committee was hoping to "adjust" in 1962 through policy changes involved New

Deal programs and, consequently, the egalitarian method of wealth distribution that Grandpa Sam and Dad supported so fervently. It is this abandoning of New Deal policies that I have experienced most of my adult life. One outcome: the U.S. Department of Agriculture reports that the number of North Dakota farms stood at fifty-three thousand in 1962, compared to about thirty thousand farms in 2002. The number of farms lost during this period represents about 43 percent of the 1962 total. To that 1962 CED committee and all its subsequent corporate accomplices, I say, mission accomplished, and then some.

The CED committee's implication in 1962 was that the free market, like an intergalactic spaceship, could more efficiently transport Americans to a future boasting an economic system fundamentally rational in how it distributed wealth. With respect to its belief of marketplace marvels, the committee already had allies: for one, Earl Butz, secretary of agriculture during the Nixon administration. Butz is linked with the admonition to "get big or get out." Certainly, bigness can produce efficiency through economies of scale—that is, farmers can spread their fixed expenses across more acres. Of course, this worship of so-called rational economic principles leads to yet another question: how does one acquire more land? The answer in many cases, remarkably, is by coveting one's neighbor's farm.

The procession of free-market policies attracted new believers in the early 1980s with the advent of the Reagan administration's "trickle down" economics. After observing free trade agreements burgeon for nearly two decades, I've concluded that the creation of a free market is by no means a hands-off undertaking. Government officials, both elected and appointed, along with nongovernmental organizations, have bargained away democratic choice, even national sovereignty itself. How national sovereignty is being sacrificed on the altar of "free" trade is exposed in chapter 11 of the North American Free Trade Agreement (NAFTA).

NAFTA and subsequent agreements have charted a trade route for U.S.-based corporations that allows a straight shot to the cheapest commodities, labor, and other inputs of all kinds from across the globe. Corporate officers following this path can now hoard profits in a manner as unrestrained as the way in which ruling despots grab political and military power.

Because of agreements such as NAFTA, multinational conglomerates are now free, through outsourcing, to hire three professionals for the price of one in many countries or to use the so-called farms race in a way that threatens the essence of America's self-sufficiency. If being able to feed its citizens through domestic production is a country's wall of defense, then any policy encouraging food imports to advance free trade guarantees an outcome akin to opening the gates to accept a gift horse. This latter example of free-market sentimentalism is backwardly feudal in that it benefits only corporations.

Disheartened citizens (of the flesh-and-bones variety) may want to ask themselves this question: is there any difference between selfish economic determinism and institutionalized theft? Recall the CED's criterion of "concern for the general welfare," and then consider the likes of Charles Keating, whose infamy links with the savings and loan scandal of the late 1980s. Or, Michael Milken, former junk bond king (now barred from the securities business for life). Or, the cochairs of corporate malfeasance: Jeffrey Skilling of Enron infamy and Dennis Kozlowski, former chief executive of Tyco. And last but certainly not least, James Cayne, former CEO of the now defunct Bear Stearns, who allegedly fiddled with his pastime for bridge while his company burned.

Decades have passed since I was a seven-year-old farm boy daydreaming about new cars and futuristic structures. What I desire today is neither a frame-off restoration of a 1962 Ford Galaxie 500 nor the stellar optimism it inspired, but rather a more hopeful, sustainable future for those still residing in rural America, and for those who want to reside there. A future, for example, absent the ghettoizing effects of methamphetamine labs.

While pondering the future, I'm also considering the past and how North Dakota's NPL party, fired by grass-roots activism, succeeded in quickly ushering in radical policy changes aimed at protecting the many instead of the few. Listen. History is knocking on our collective door, and the message it wants to deliver is this: populism is an effective counterbalance to corporate greed.

Existing only in memory is the barbershop of my youth. Also gone are two of the three grocery stores, the hardware store, a repair shop, the machinist, the lumber-yard, the drugstore, the car and machinery dealerships, rail service, and nearly half the people, including me, for whom the decision to leave was a matter of choice, one that nonetheless offers little consolation on many days. While I accept the reality of never being able to go home again in a figurative sense, I discount the lie that claims the death of my hometown is inevitable. And so, I will continue fighting any policy or economic scheme purporting to be rational when it is only calculating.

Instead of pioneering new frontiers of prosperity for rural America, the free market, as in all gilded ages, has become a juggernaut, perpetuating an ages-old cruelty rooted in arrogance and greed and guaranteeing prosperity for a predetermined few. The time has come for state and federal policy makers—once again—to exorcise that arrogance and greed before even more Americans are unwillingly plucked from the countryside by the invisible hand of an economic system that draws from a stacked deck. The course of events leading away from 1962 clearly demonstrates that a free market doesn't exist for family farmers, and this fact, more than any other, is responsible for the depopulation of North Dakota's countryside and moreover, the evisceration of America's agricultural heartland.

And so, having government at all levels prepared to intervene against single-minded interests hell-bent on maximizing profits is as necessary as rainfall and the seasons of the year. This lesson has become my inheritance, and it remains a lesson for future generations to learn as well, unless we truly have become complacent enough to accept as reality a deserted, dysfunctional rural American landscape capable of producing crops, for a time, but no more culture.

Rocks Taking Root

When I yanked rocks from our farm fields as a teenager in the early 1970s, my thoughts consisted mostly of complaints about the work's drudgery and fears of unearthing a shade-seeking snake. At no time do I recall considering why any rock lay as it did, let alone whether hands were involved in its placement.

In 2004 I was being compelled by connectedness the day I set out to rediscover the homestead remnants of my maternal great-great-grandparents. The Ryders, Alfred and Annie, had emigrated from England to Canada and then to Richburg Township in North Dakota's Bottineau County. Their homestead claim, filed in 1895, was for a chunk of land lying along the west bank of the Souris River. As demarcated by the U.S. Public Land Survey System, their homestead was located in Section 13 of Township 163 North, Range 80 West.

On the day of my trek, the greens of summer already were yielding to the yellows, reds, and browns of autumn. A thunderstorm had passed and the downpour's aftermath turned from light drizzle to mist. Eastbound, I strode among the grasses on a prairie trail and studied the shelterbelts to my right, rows of trees perpendicular to the lane spaced about an eighth of a mile apart. My knowledge of this landscape's history informed me that many of the trees were only a generation older than I.

However, I hadn't hunted upland game and water-fowl near this particular spot since my youth, and so the images I was encountering appeared new, momentarily, but then a jolt of recognition generated a memory. Beside the sixty-foot cottonwood trees near a barbed wire fence, I spotted Dr. Greene's gravel pit. Images of the red leather furniture adorning his four-room office flashed into my mind, as it always does when I think of Doc, who died before I turned eight. Doc owned nearby farmland, as well as a dark blue Cadillac with a baby blue top—the only Cadillac in town at the time. He was an investor in the countryside as well as the community, my hometown's last lifelong medical practitioner. My eyes again fixed on the man-made undulations, now grown over with grasses and leafy spurge, and I realized that it had been decades since any gravel left that pit.

Leafy spurge is a noxious weed, and by late summer its once lime green flowers, having matured throughout the growing season, acquire a muted yellow hue; its latex-laden stems and leaves, which cattle refuse to eat, become mottled with brown and traces of black. Leafy spurge immigrated to the United States and Canada with northern European settlers in bags of seed and other conveyances. As settlers plowed and replanted the Great Plains prairie to cereal grains and nonnative grasses, leafy spurge spread as fast as the hope preceding its introduction, perhaps even more quickly than the frustration following its establishment.

What is it about human history, my own included, that disappoints me? I focused on white settlement and the various human cohorts that had imposed their greed, arrogance, and ignorance on this part of the world: the fur traders, the railroad barons, the bison hunters, the land speculators, the policy makers, the settlers themselves.

Suddenly, I saw two large, brown eyes and equally oversized ears. A fawn had arisen from its grassy-weedy resting place and was watching me. Later, I compared my experience to that of Adam's—me, attempting to name what I saw. The face of innocence? Of peacefulness? Or was it the face of conscience asking me why I'd been away so long?

While I was in the moment, the fawn broke any chance to contemplate. It offered a questioning bleat, and then began approaching with a jerky, instinctively cautious movement. I stood still until the small animal was about thirty yards away. Transfixed, and oddly afraid that the animal might actually walk right up to me, I spoke, flippantly: "I'm not your mom," my words stopping the fawn in its tracks, then turning it, sending it fleeing.

My visit came at the end of August—one of the coldest on record. Thoughts about cold weather, loneliness, and despair flooded my mind as I began my gradual north-by-northeast descent along the riverbank to where I hoped to find evidence of a stone house and barn: the Ryder farmstead, which local amateur historians, a husband and wife and former neighbors of mine, called a "showplace."

Relying on general directions from the couple, other friends, and relatives who themselves had not visited the site for years or even decades, I continued walking, tripping, and stumbling on the slick and profuse leafy spurge until I thought I'd gone too far. Early on, my Red Wing boots had begun sloughing off the moisture that the saturated leather could no longer absorb. My gray cotton socks, also soaked, contributed to the squish-squishing sound my movement produced, and my blue jeans, wet from the knees down, clung to my legs like staticky silk, and sticking to the denim were hundreds of grass seeds.

Just as I had convinced myself to try again the following spring, when the weather would be nicer but the wood ticks copious, I fixed my gaze on a few stunted trees. Markers of human presence? Like the curious fawn's, my instinct ultimately prevailed. As I approached the trees, obscurity gave way and I saw four stone "columns," two of which I took to be the northwest and northeast corners of the barn, and the others, a center portion of the house.

Alfred Ryder died in 1916, and the twenty-one-year span between when he had filed his homestead claim and his death were not altogether kind to him and Annie. During my adolescence, all I learned of my great-great-grandparents came from Mom, who told me that Alfred was a stonemason and had worked on several buildings in Bottineau County, including the barn on the farmstead where his daughter, Rachel, my great-grandmother, had lived as an adult. As for Annie, Mom said she had been a "fancy cook" in England. Every time Mom mentioned Granny Ryder after I'd seen the film *Remains of the Day*, I pictured the kitchen scene where women in white caps and aprons moved nonstop amid roaring fires and steaming cauldrons of food. The only other lore Mom retold about the Ryders was that Alfred had been a kind man, but one prone to episodes of uncontrolled drinking, during which he squandered hard-earned wages.

The tales of Alfred's alcoholism came to Mom from her mother, my grandma Trimble, who had learned of Alfred's drinking through firsthand experience, as well as from stories from her mother, Rachel. I suspect it was this experience that Mom used as the basis for her generalization about this or that person from our community being "nothing but a darned old alcoholic."

Likewise, other family members can add only anecdotal detail to further expose the contrast of Alfred's personality. A female cousin from Mom's generation confirms that he liked his liquor. She says he had a still on a neighbor's property in Richburg Township. Once, while working in Bottineau, about thirty miles to the east, he learned that the police were planning a raid, so he rode his horse hard to arrive ahead of the law and save the still. He succeeded.

Alfred and his family first settled near Toronto, where Alfred helped construct government buildings before moving on to homestead near Reston, Manitoba. Alfred came to Canada ahead of his family because the police in England were after him. My cousin writes, "It sounds like he was always in a fight over something or other."

Rachel's husband, Cassius Anor Matthews, had to take his father-in-law to Bottineau several times to dry him out in the local jail. My cousin's father told her that Alfred often required a "nip" to cut the dust in his throat put there by stonemasonry. Alfred somehow mixed nipping with loving his children and grandchildren, including those who hadn't survived childhood. In the small Coultervale Cemetery just north of the U.S.–Canada border stand four hand-carved tombstones marking the graves of four of Alfred and Annie's grandchilden. Alfred carved these and other tombstones in the Coultervale Cemetery and in various cemeteries extending up to Brandon, Manitoba.

As I walked about the homestead, I marveled at the size of the fieldstones that Alfred had selected for his barn.

Not stones, really. Small boulders, some, easily weighing several hundred pounds or more, heavy enough to require real horsepower and a block and tackle to put in place. I speculated about Alfred's tools: chisels, hammers, punches, mallets, handsaws.

In writing about the meaning of tools, essayist Donovan Hohn compares the harmony between a craftsman and his tools to that which existed between Adam and the beasts. Hohn suggests that Americans are experiencing an "epidemic frustration" because of our need to make things. In his novel *Hannah Coulter*, Wendell Berry has his narrator describe her son, Caleb, as being disappointed in himself for not loving farming enough to become a farmer, but also for loving it too much to be completely happy doing the work he chose. She says, "There is the same kind of apology in him that you see in some of the sweeter drunks." I imagine Alfred Ryder as having been that type of conflicted apologist. If so, it's a feeling I share with this long-lost relative.

My reason for believing Alfred may not have loved stonemasonry enough is based on a Ryder clan story, now generations old. Alfred's father, Joseph, and Joseph's brother, Jacob, had a Protestant father and a Catholic mother who had agreed to let their boys attend the church of their choice until Joseph, the youngest, turned fourteen. Then, their mother offered to split her wealth evenly between the two boys if they agreed to become Catholic. Only Jacob agreed, and so he became sole inheritor. Like his father, Joseph became a marble sculptor—and embittered—so much so that he tried to instill his hatred of Catholics into his ten children, six of whom were boys. Joseph's eldest son, Bill, preached against Catholicism in the streets of his village until someone murdered him. Alfred and his brother Albert were the only sons to stick with stonemasonry, even though Joseph had required all his sons to learn the trade before embarking on other vocations.

When I'm imagining Alfred as apologist, I see his hands: rough, calloused, split nails, perhaps, greasy dirt, like ink, embedded deeply into cracks and pores. Besides the dust, stonemasonry, then and now, must be back-wrenching work, with its requirement of contortion for working in tight quarters. Stonemasonry also is meticulous work, and therefore it must be satisfying. Stonemasons must be passionate, like all artists. Proud, too. And so I hope for Alfred's sake that along with the passion and the pride came enough peace to smooth the roughest edges of his disappointment.

In the 1940s, Mom and Dad bought a quarter section of land that Nicki and I now own. Technically, it is the southeast quarter of Section 15 (Township 163 North, Range 80 West), about a mile west of the Ryder homestead. The original plat map of Richburg Township shows a squiggly line bisecting the cube of land into nearly perfect right triangles. My former neighbors, the amateur historians, told me that the line represents an American Indian route, according to a Canadian historian they interviewed.

Similarly, the journals of François-Antoine Larocque and Alexander Henry the Younger, both circa 1805, contain maps depicting their trade excursions into the area, and both place them in the vicinity of present-day Richburg Township. So perhaps the line on the plat map does indeed represent a trade route. In his journal, Larocque describes encounters with the Assiniboine:

[W]e had not been 2 hours encamped, when three, and soon after many other Assiniboins rushed in upon us, a few endeavoring to take our horses, but seizing our guns and running to them we made them dep[a]rt. They came afterwards to our fire and se[e]ing us well armed, and by our looks that we would well defend ourselves and our property they remained quiet. There were 40 Tent of them not 10 acres from us without that we had perceived them.

He also tells of his camping along the Souris River in a place with no "wood on its side for about 30 miles." This encampment could have been where the Souris flows north through Bottineau County. It might have been on the very land that became my great-great-grandparents' homestead. If so, Larocque enjoyed a panoramic view of Turtle Mountain, thirty miles to the east.

In 1887 Congress failed to appropriate any money to aid the Turtle Mountain Ojibwe, even though federal lawmakers earmarked three thousand dollars in 1886 and 1888, respectively, and then five thousand dollars in 1889. This failure resulted in the deaths, from starvation, of 151 Turtle Mountain Ojibwe. On a memorial marking this tragedy appears the following, from tribal historian Charlie White Weasel: "This is just one result of the U.S. government policy of ethnic genocide applied to force Indian surrender."

Even though the U.S. Department of the Interior's General Land Office opened Bottineau County for homesteading in the early 1890s, it was about a decade later when the Turtle Mountain Ojibwe ratified the treaty ceding land including present-day Richburg Township. Like Alfred Ryder, many of the northern European homesteaders who settled in Richburg Township along the Souris

River lost their farms to foreclosure. Legal documents show that Alfred and Annie bought their homestead back, and bought more land, too, but eventually, the land went to the government—this time, the state of North Dakota, the holder of a mortgage for five thousand dollars dating back to 1909.

The day I visited the Ryder homestead, I was vaguely aware of the 1887 Ojibwe deaths, but I knew nothing about the treaty or my great-great-grandparents' legal and financial wranglings. I had come to see the stones Alfred had sculpted and reacquaint myself with the place. A cousin told me that my great-grandmother Rachel many times rode in the wagon with her father when he hauled stones from Turtle Mountain. I had wondered what Alfred thought of the various stone formations he might have encountered on his treks across the mountain: cairns, sight lines marking solstices and equinoxes.

My fear is that because of his experiences with the so-called troubles between Protestants and Catholics in Great Britain, Alfred carried prejudices even more defined than my own, which I hope education has abraded. But then, I may be giving myself too much credit because when it comes to human emotion, education is often no match for firsthand experience.

What did Alfred Ryder think of Catholics? More to the point, what did he think of the Ojibwe, whose spirituality originated from rootstock other than Christianity and whose cultural history, in part, lay spread across Turtle Mountain? Did he ever consider that his homestead once had been Ojibwe land? Probably not, because treaties, and the paper upon which the apparently agreeable words appear, imply legality and thereby fairness. Would Alfred have disturbed the rock formations? Perhaps, if a particular rock held appeal. But I have my doubts about whether an artisan would steal the work of another, regardless of spiritual differences, or worse yet, bury it amid the concrete of his own creation.

Through long-ago emigration, a decision the English (under King James I) forced, some of the Turnbull clan moved from Scotland to what is today Northern Ireland and became the "Trimble" clan, and then the more adventuresome ones moved to America generations later. Through migration to North Dakota, the Ryders and my branch of the Trimbles (Iowans) ended up in Richburg Township. My Protestant Scotch-Irish heritage and my birthplace—that is, my respective genealogical and geographical relationships with British and U.S. histories—have led me to conclude that colonialism links Irish Catholics with American Indians. Both experienced occupation, dependency, starvation, and other forms of premeditated murder. Both became the "other," beings not on a par with their oppressors and thus deserving castigation by way of cultural castration.

There is no record of pre-Christian Celtic tribes having a creation story. One possible reason for this mythological dearth may lie with sixth- and seventh-century monastic scholars who wove the Christian version into Irish history, writes Proinsias MacCana in *Celtic Mythology*. In contrast, ethnologist Basil Johnston teaches that Ojibwe mythology does contain a creation story, in which Kitche Manitou (the Great Spirit) created rock, water, fire, and wind from nothing. Into each, he breathed a different essence and nature so that each possessed power—that is, a soul-spirit.

Both the Irish and the Ojibwe have flood stories. According to Celtic legend, all perished in the flood except Fintan, whose long life and many experiences resulted from his ability to assume various animal forms: a salmon, an eagle, and a hawk. Ojibwe mythology tells of a flood wiping out everything except the water animals, birds, and fish, which pitied the lonely sky-woman spirit. The animals convinced a turtle to rise to the surface of the waters and offer his back as a haven for the sky-woman, who accepted the invitation. The sky-woman asked the animals to gather soil from the bottom of the sea. Many tried and failed and finally the muskrat volunteered and succeeded. The sky-woman painted the rim of the turtle's back with the morsel of soil and breathed life into it. Because of its service, the turtle became the interpreter of thought and feelings so that beings of all kinds could communicate. The day I visited the homestead of ancestors I never knew, I was attempting to discover what the landscape, vis-à-vis Turtle Mountain, was saying to me.

The land once owned by Alfred and Annie Ryder, along with most of the land on both sides of the Souris River extending fifty miles southward from the U.S.–Canada border, became what today is called the J. Clark Salyer National Wildlife Refuge, North Dakota's largest, encompassing 58,700 acres. In other words, homesteads such as that of my immigrant great-great-grandparents became federal land once again, and now serve as sanctuary for animals of the water and of flight—beings, too, that migrate to survive.

Were the settlers of my great-great-grandparents' generation set up to fail? Sans hindsight, the answer depends on whom one believed at the time. After the Civil

War, there were divergent opinions concerning the Great Plains' potential, and some debate centered on meridians of longitude.

Of particular interest was the one hundredth meridian, which slices through Turtle Mountain. The embodiment of a boldly optimistic Great Plains perspective was William Gilpin, a friend of presidents ranging from Jackson to Lincoln, who is portrayed by Wallace Stegner in *Beyond the Hundredth Meridian:*

> [Gilpin] saw the West through a blaze of mystical fervor, as part of a grand geopolitical design, the overture to global harmony; and his conception of its resources and its future as a home for millions was as grandiose as his rhetoric, as unlimited as his faith, as splendid as his capacity for inaccuracy. . . . Gilpin joined the politicians and the railroads, eager for settlers, in finding most of the plains region exuberantly arable. . . . And on these plains, once the wild herds were exterminated, three domestic animals could be pastured where one wild one had formerly roamed.

As hindsight reveals, many of Gilpin's claims were as wild as the bison he encouraged Americans to displace so brutally, and his drunken optimism proved to be as reckless as those who hunted the bison to near extinction.

Holding a contrasting view to that mouthed by Gilpin was John Wesley Powell, an explorer of the American West who, on August 5, 1889, shared his thoughts on water with delegates attending the North Dakota constitutional convention:

> Eastern Dakota, he said, nearly always had enough rain, central Dakota sometimes did, and western Dakota practically

never did. Both the eastern belt, with adequate rainfall, and the western, which had to depend completely on irrigation, were safe. The danger lay in the middle. . . . He meant that central Dakota was what the British in India called a "famine belt," though he had the political sense not to use that phrase. . . . When rain failed in a region that had made no preparations against drouth, failure was complete.

Stegner's reportage, coming nearly seven decades after the fact, stands as a tribute to Powell's clear-eyed prophecy.

As I walked on the refuge amid the rubble of Alfred and Annie's barn that August day in 2004, the Souris River and Turtle Mountain dominated the eastern view. Once, I stumbled when my slick-soled boot skidded across the top of one of Alfred's wet stones. I started to fall, but caught myself, even though the maneuver caused my spine's L-5 vertebra and its bone spurs to remind me with sharp, shocking pain that I now possessed the arthritis and rheumatism that hobbled Mom, her sisters, and Grandma Trimble for much of their lives. As I lurched forward, then back, my camera bumped against my chest. I'd placed it underneath the yellow rubber slicker I was wearing to protect it from the mist. Sensing the camera against my chest reminded me of Jack London's short story "To Build a Fire" and the ignorant, arrogant voyager, with his grease-sopped biscuits placed against his body to avoid freezing.

After I had righted myself, I studied the eastern horizon beyond the river and saw a grain truck traveling along what I knew to be a gravel road. I was confident that the driver could see me. Aside from protection against rain, I'd chosen my slicker to stand out against the landscape, not so much to aid rescuers (like London's voyager, I hadn't considered needing rescue), but rather to convince any unseen onlookers that I was not a homeland security threat, given my proximity to the U.S.–Canada border.

I watched the truck become a speck in the distance and understood then that I was quite alone. I took this collection of thoughts and observations to be one of the landscape's messages: for the experienced, being absolutely alone with nature yields tranquillity, but disquiet for the unpracticed or the out of practice.

Being so focused on my own frailty and mortality, I was slow to take comfort in ethnologist Basil Johnston's words about the Ojibwe belief that rock endures: "All else changes; earth remains unchanging and continues to give life. It is a promise to the future, to those yet to be born." Perhaps, even, to those wishing to be born again into a spiritualism more linked to land. As those thoughts flooded my consciousness, I continued exploring the farmstead. The longer I stayed, the more at home I felt.

Rocks I picked as a farm boy now function as rectangles, circles, and the other geometric designs composing the landscape Nicki and I created outside our home in Fargo. Most of these rocks came from a pile about one mile west of the Ryder homestead and were free, except for the gasoline my pickup drank on the five 600-mile round-trips from Fargo to our farm. Some of these rocks are especially pretty: one rock, pink with quartz sparkles.

I am beginning to believe these rocks can heal. About a month after my visit to the Ryder homestead, I spent the better part of a sparkling fall day in our backyard preparing our gardens for winter. I engaged that day in what has become a decades-old annual ritual: mourning our inability to savor the aroma of burning leaves within Fargo city limits. While I was fantasizing about life in the country-side, my aches and pains abated, and my spirit lifted. Perhaps the sunshine and its accompanying warmth aided me. Or maybe transplanted rocks eventually regrow roots of memory. I hope.

In her memoir *Wild Stone Heart*, Sharon Butala laments the loss of stone formations, many of which were centuries—perhaps millennia—old:

> How strange it was that the settlers, my own people on both sides, too, could not *see* what was there all over the prairie. They'd used the stones to build dams and for foundations for their buildings . . . they were dismantling the remains of a civilization. Every stone freighted with tears, with the weight of grief, they should have been too heavy to lift.

Likewise, those who scavenged the lumber and most of the stones from the Ryder homestead probably thought little about the efforts and dreams that had preceded theirs. So march the superstitions of progress.

And yet, some of the stones my great-great-grandfather honed a half century before I was born remain snuggly embedded in concrete in a place where deer sleep, mostly undisturbed, on the grounds of a watery refuge teeming with other wildlife symbolizing resiliency. To the east stands Turtle Mountain, a mythological monument to second chances, thereby implying that the materials for miracles lie just a stone's throw away.

The Past
Is Close Behind

Before dinner sometimes Grandpa Sam Hulse and I went on drives in our cow pasture. Our course took us by five cottonwood trees next to a barbed wire fence that separated the pasture from Dad's alfalfa field. On occasion, Grandpa Sam parked his car in the midday shade, and we watched the cattle amble. If we stayed too long, Spike, our border collie, checked on us. Then the three of us headed to the house for dinner, with Spike leading the way. Our trips through the pasture produced a prairie trail perfectly matched to the width of the car's wheels. That path melted into grass after the winter of my first sorrow, the year Grandpa Sam died.

Because I was only five when he died, my memories of driving with Grandpa Sam come wrapped in a cottony vagueness. Clearer is the recollection of a summer Sunday morning when Mom and Dad had gone to church and left Grandpa Sam in charge. He told me not to leave the fenced-in portion of our farmyard, but I opened the gate anyway and headed out for adventure. My destination: the swather Dad had parked in the shade of some box elders on the south side of our farmstead near a drainage ditch that wound its way east to the Souris River. Within a matter of minutes I'd become entangled among slats of wood in the swather's reel.

When Grandpa Sam noticed where I was, he yelled from the back stoop, "Goddamn ye, young'un, get back in the house."

I had never heard a harsh word come from Grandpa Sam before, not even when I'd once wet the bed, which disrupted his night's sleep because we slept together. I untangled myself and got back in the house lickety-split. Grandpa Sam's family moved to North Dakota in 1909 from an Illinois farm of about 250 acres near a town called Oblong. I don't know how many generations of Hulses farmed before Andrew Jackson "Jack" Hulse, my great-great-grandfather, but my generation of Hulses most likely will be the last to hold a memory of the land, and I want mine to be as rich as possible. I've traveled to Oblong, and on a sticky summer day I stood on reddish brown Illinois soil that other Hulses had once trod upon, where a century earlier Grandpa Sam no doubt had sought shade from the swelter. I was gazing at a landscape Dad had never seen, and as I looked off across a field of supple soybeans, heat rose from the land in waves, like history.

The first Hulse farm in North Dakota lay about eight miles north and west of Westhope. All that farmland was physically joined, one piece to another, like branches to a tree trunk. I'm guessing that for Oscar Monroe ("O. M.") Hulse, my great-grandpa, the farm's configuration was a key reason for buying it, because land scattered across the countryside means spending precious time moving machinery from one place to another.

O. M. died thirty-one years before I was born, and so I can't know what he saw when he first laid eyes on the canvas of his North Dakota farm. But in a different era I've seen a prairie landscape become a moving picture as a crop of wheat or barley or oats emerges from blackened soil, its greenery waving, teasing in the wind. What follows is the staged accumulation of more new leaves and eventually stems and kernels—all finally acquiring a golden hue and all the while promising with a whisper: this might be the year.

Dad specially ordered our 1960 Oldsmobile, which came without a radio—"to avoid the fights," he said. Even though I was only five at the time, I wondered, "What fights?" I came to understand that Mom and Dad were, in many ways, just like all couples, disagreements included. However, I learned that theirs was a life containing some unusual aspects, one of which was their shared emotional burden of having lost two daughters before I was born. Another was getting what they'd wished for—me—when they both were only months shy of turning forty, with all the ingrained habits and encroaching physical changes that middle age implies.

Until he died, Grandpa Sam had lived with Mom and Dad for their entire marriage. When they married, Grandpa Sam already had been a widower for more than two decades and was nearing retirement. I have the sense that Mom became testier after Grandpa Sam died, and perhaps even testier still two years later when she lost her own father, Elmer Trimble. I believe Mom was left feeling simultaneously freer and sadder, which is how I felt after losing Dad and her.

I'm more than willing to accept my share of blame for the screaming sessions that ensued when I was a hormone-charged teenager, but I can't convince myself that at age eight, nine, or even ten, I was truly evil enough to require reforming. And yet, one summer Sunday Dad threatened to send me to reform school.

As had become the routine, I stayed on Friday and Saturday with Mom's sister Aunt Goldie and her family at their cabin on Bottineau County's Lake Metigoshe. On Sunday, Mom and Dad, along with Grandma Trimble (by then a widow), had driven up from Westhope. I don't recall how I had managed to get into an argument with Mom, or even what the argument was about. All I remember is complaining to Dad about the unfairness of the situation after we fell off a homemade plywood surfboard we'd been riding. Clad in life jackets, we dog-paddled as the boat circled around so we could recommence our surfing. As we waited, I renewed my complaints against Mom by asking a question I often posed: "Why does Mom have to be the way she is?"

This time, however, Dad said, "If you don't shape up, we're going to send you to reform school."

I knew about reform school—that is, the state industrial school—because a ne'er-do-well from Westhope had recently gone there after getting caught breaking into the clothing store. I thought for a minute about living far away from home with boys such as our local thief. Even scarier, knowing that the person floating alongside me, the one I trusted most in the world, had just betrayed me. Furthermore, he had the power to transform threats into actions. Suddenly, Lake Metigoshe became the Pacific Ocean, and I was a speck on the water.

Instead of the reform school threat, I had been expecting Dad to say, "At least you have a mother." This was his pat response, often followed by, "Tell Mom you're sorry."

So many times I remember apologizing to Mom for an argument that had begun with what I saw as her irrational reaction to something I'd done, or not done.

Dad lost his mom when he was five, the reason I believe he accommodated Mom's wishes on many matters, particularly on the subject of Mother's Day itself. As a child, I dreaded Mother's Day because it meant I'd be the only one my age wearing a carnation to church. Always a red carnation because my mother was living, unlike Dad, whose white carnation symbolized his loss. Back then, I thought Dad's flower should have been pinned on his sleeve instead of a lapel.

It was years later before I fully grasped the irony of Dad's motherlessness. Aunt Sylvia, Grandpa Sam's half sister, childless herself, had taken on the role of surrogate to Dad and his siblings, along with a fatherless first cousin and at least one other unrelated family of motherless boys. My memories of Sylvia center on her sure-as-the-sun-comes-up-in-the-east greeting as I walked into her home, always unannounced because I never knocked. I never took more than a few steps inside her home before I heard her footsteps followed by the confirming joyfulness of "Well, Dean."

Before I was old enough to do any unsupervised farmwork, I spent many summer hours in our black pickup truck: daydreaming about food or cars or toys or whatever; rummaging through the glove box; staring at passersby—anything I could think of to fight off the boredom. Meanwhile, Dad whiled away hour after hour visiting at a local café or the barbershop, a habit he'd honed during the decade most of our farmland had lain idle when it was in the Soil Bank program. Dad told friends that he'd enrolled our farm so that he could spend more time with me as I was growing up. Once I could drive a tractor without supervision, Dad assigned me odd jobs such as picking rock. For this type of work I used our International Harvester "M," which was so old that the red paint had faded to a rusty brown hue. Because our M didn't have a front-end loader, rock picking on the Hulse farm also required a stoneboat, a four-by-eight-foot piece of reinforced plywood mounted on skids and capable of sliding along the ground when a tractor of sufficient horsepower was pulling it. I had to pick and place each rock on the stoneboat, mount the tractor, drive it (towing the stoneboat) to the rock pile, dismount, lift a rock off the stoneboat, and throw it onto the pile. And then repeat the lifting and throwing until the stoneboat was empty. Manual labor, with as much conversation as one could expect during a church service, say a funeral.

When I was in high school, Dad had a local carpenter build us a machine shed set on a forty-by-eighty-foot concrete slab. I remember one August morning, around eight o'clock, when the air still felt cool and pleasant. Experience told me, however, that before too long the combination of heat and humidity would melt my comfort. Nevertheless, Dad decided it was a good day to sweep the floor of our new shed. My tool for this task was a push broom shorter than three feet wide. When Dad came home from town for dinner, I was sweaty and muddy from the dust I'd disturbed, but I'd finished my job. Dad gazed across the virtually spotless concrete floor and said, "I didn't expect you to do this good of a job."

Dad's response was as typical as it was frustrating, and it stood in stark contrast to what Mom's response might have been, had she offered one. She most likely would have found something wrong with my effort. I'm not a student of Calvinism and the so-called Protestant work ethic, but I learned from observing Mom, as she raised a profusion of flowers and vegetables and then turned both into prize-winning bouquets and delicious foods, that hard work and discipline—that is, perfection—were goals to shoot for, if not attain.

Having parents who, respectively, were relaxed and hard charging, lenient and rigid, made for some perplexing lessons, and being an only child often made this situation more confused in that it yielded more questions than answers. It is this incessant mental threshing of wheat from chaff that has informed many of my life's decisions, good and bad.

Nicki and I farmed near Westhope for two seasons, the first of which was in 1978. I planted wheat, barley, and oats, in that order. The wheat wasn't out of the ground too far before Dad pointed out the yellowish tint appearing between the rows. Yield-stealing pigeongrass. I informed my uncle Cliff (married to Mom's sister Goldie), because I was renting a quarter section of his land where a pigeongrass stand was promising to be a bumper crop, and our rental agreement was based on crop share, not cash rent. Uncle Cliff was a retired civil servant who had moved back to Westhope so that he could be more involved with farming. He knew there wasn't much we could do about the pigeongrass. We talked in vain about the herbicide Hoelon, which could have killed it. Trouble was, U.S. regulations didn't yet allow American farmers to use Hoelon, even though our Canadian neighbors just a few miles to the north could.

I could have run a light, spring-tooth harrow over the wheat ground and killed many of the shallow-rooted pigeongrass plants, but Dad didn't own the implement we needed, and neither Cliff nor Dad nor I wanted to damage the wheat plants, or to dry out the sandy soil and create a second problem: wind erosion. So I decided to sit tight and hope that the wheat plants outcompeted the pigeongrass for nutrients and moisture.

For much of the early part of that summer, a gentle rain fell about once a week and generally showered the land with an inch, or thereabouts. The wheat grew lush, as did the barley and the oats. One Sunday afternoon, the local banker drove by one of my fields and later told Dad he'd never seen a better crop of oats. After harvest, Cliff's friend, a local elevator manager, found a market for our oats in California—racehorses and we pocketed a premium price. Likewise, our barley crop yielded higher than average.

When the wheat finally headed out, I thought we had beaten the pigeongrass. For about a week, the crop on Cliff's quarter section looked picture perfect. But the spring wheat I had grown that year was shorter than conventional varieties, and once the pigeongrass reached its full height, it stretched taller than the wheat. A bumper crop one day—a mess within a week.

The day combining began, I was nervous and excited. We had traded Dad's combine on a new twenty-four-foot swather and a used tractor and had hired custom combiners. I had imagined Dad and me riding together in the pickup, having discussions before making harvesting decisions. I expected to learn a lot, but when I went to the house to get Dad, Mom told me he'd decided to drive to Glenburn to retrieve our grain auger, which had been damaged in a summer windstorm.

"Goddamn it! What did he do that for?" I yelled. "He knows we don't need that damned auger today." Mom began crying, and I was shocked, and saddened, by our role reversals. At the same time, I saw in my mind's eye the taillights of Dad's pickup, just as I'd witnessed for years, and I inferred that he was off on yet another venture to get out of some work.

Earlier, Dad and I had had an argument about the auger. The insurance settlement allowed us to buy a replacement. I wanted to spend more than the insurance money and buy a larger auger, one with an eight-inch diameter capable of moving more grain, faster. Instead, Dad wanted to fix the auger and save a few hundred dollars.

Dad didn't return from Glenburn, only fifty miles away, until late afternoon, by which time a thunderstorm had halted work. It wasn't until he got home that he thought to start the auger to see how it worked. It didn't. The screw was still warped enough that it rubbed against the tube, and the engine wasn't powerful enough to overcome the friction. Next day, Dad wasted several more hours taking the auger back to Glenburn. When he got home, he said the auger wouldn't be ready until after harvest.

Determined not to let Dad again sidestep his role as mentor, I became his taskmaster, asking Mom where he was or interrogating Dad as to where he was going. Even if it killed both of us, I was determined to learn.

The wheat on Cliff's land was the last crop we har-
vested, and Cliff dropped by to check on progress as
we were finishing up. I said, "The wheat should run
about thirty-five bushels to the acre. That's pretty damn
good."

To that, Cliff responded, "Yeah, but your pigeongrass
ran about fifty bushels to the acre."

I knew then my wheat crop wasn't perfect, although it
took many more years for me to realize that my failures,
perceived and real, produce fear and anger. When Cliff
condemned my farming, I didn't understand. Later that
same day, Dad and I got into an argument (the subject of
which I've long since forgotten) as we were hauling a load
of pigeongrass screenings for feeding sparrows, thrushes,
and other birds. We were passengers in the same old black
pickup truck in which I had whiled away so many boring
hours in my youth. I don't remember the last insult Dad
leveled at me. I do recall my reaction: an uncontrollable
desire to hit back at him with my most hurtful, frightful
memory. I reminded Dad that he'd once threatened to
send me to reform school.

"That's a goddamned lie," he said.

The sense of betrayal I felt all those years ago when
he and I were surfboarding came back to me—so fresh I
could nearly splash the lake water. When I reoriented my
thoughts to the present, I was staring into Dad's angry
face, a stranger once again. As if it had suddenly been
programmed to produce pain, my mind flashed to more
traumatic childhood scenes: images of Mom hitting me
with the flyswatter for "sassing" her, of Mom chasing
me through the house to mete out her punishment, of
Mom's foreboding scowl. In a rage fueled by recollections

of childhood injustices, I supplied Dad with specific details about the lake, the surfboard.

"That's a pretty good memory for a goddamned liar, isn't it?" And then I absorbed the silent aftermath, our unspoken agreement that we'd gone too far. Nicki and I were living in Fargo by the time harvest had come again.

Dad told me the story many times. A heart attack killed O. M. Hulse, my great-grandpa. After eating a meal, he simply walked into the living room, sat in his favorite chair, and never got up.

Like his dad, Grandpa Sam died from a heart attack, but in a hospital, on a mid-September day in a year that had brought abundant moisture and, subsequently, a second cutting of hay. Dad quit baling early that day so we could drive the sixty miles to Minot and see Grandpa Sam, who was recovering from surgery to repair a twisted bowel. Because I was too young to visit, Mom and I waited in the car. Dad had been in the hospital for only a few minutes before he came back out and told us Grandpa Sam was dead. A nurse had explained that she brought him his supper and had momentarily turned her back when she heard him make a noise. He was already dead when she turned to face him. Even before we had driven past the outdoor movie theater on Minot's north edge headed for home, I had already asked the question several times: "But why did Grandpa Sam die?"

Dad's death was complicated. Like his father, Dad was a diabetic, but unlike Grandpa Sam, the disease exacted a costly physical price from Dad, who lost a leg and some of his eyesight before a severe heart attack left him an invalid.

The doctors figured that Dad had walked around for two or three days without realizing he had had a heart attack. Dad's diabetes-damaged nerve endings couldn't signal, through pain, the trouble he was in. Only his flu-like symptoms eventually clued him in, but by then he'd sustained 55 percent heart damage, which kept him in intensive care for two weeks, then a hospital room for several more weeks, and finally a nursing home for many months.

For a brief time after he had transferred Dad from the emergency room to intensive care, the attending doctor thought Dad's heart attack had been mild. When Mom called us late on a Saturday, New Year's Eve 1988, she was calm and said there was no need for us to drive to Minot from Fargo. Agitated, she called back early the next morning after the doctor revealed Dad's blood test results.

Nicki and I got to the hospital by midafternoon. The intensive care waiting room was full of familiar faces: friends, former neighbors, Uncle Chet (Dad's brother) and Aunt Evelyn. Mom said other relatives had been calling from their winter retreats in Arizona. Mom also said that Dad didn't yet know how serious his heart attack had been. The doctor didn't want to tell him for a few days until the worst of the danger had passed. When I went in to see Dad the first time, he was lying with his arms up above his shoulders, hands locked behind his head, looking peaceful, as if nothing at all was wrong. He kept repeating, "I feel fine."

Two days later a heart surgeon convinced us that Dad's heart needed help. While Mom stayed in the intensive care waiting room, I listened as the surgeon told Dad he needed a balloon inserted into an artery near his heart. I watched Dad's facial expression when he found out that more than half his heart had been damaged. The surgeon said he would perform the procedure in twenty minutes and that Dad might die from it. As I was leaving his room, I turned back and momentarily watched Dad's chest heaving with his deep breathing, his eyes staring at the ceiling.

I stayed in the hospital for as many nights as I could during the first month after Dad's heart attack. I slept on a couch in the intensive care waiting room and then in a recliner next to Dad's bed in his private room. One night about two o'clock Dad asked me to rub some lotion on his aching back. As he was slumped forward, he grieved, like a horseman. He said, "It's been a long, hard pull."

Dad did eventually get home, but during the next several years he spent more stints in a hospital and then in a nursing home when a sore on his head wouldn't heal. Finally, Dad's kidneys failed, he was hospitalized, and then once again transferred to a nursing home. All the while, nearly two months, he was semicomatose.

Dad died in 1992 in Bottineau, in a swing bed unit, a euphemism for designated wings in underutilized rural hospitals that function as temporary nursing homes for the seriously, chronically, or terminally ill. The day Dad died, Mom had gone to Minot for a doctor's checkup and returned to Westhope by midafternoon. Mom said she had a sense that she should drive the thirty miles to Bottineau and visit Dad, even though she wouldn't get there much before five o'clock, about suppertime for those well enough to eat. Mom had been in Dad's room for about twenty minutes when he died.

My aunt Goldie called me with the news from her summer home in Westhope. I immediately called Dad's hospital room, and Mom's best friend, Hazel, answered. She said Mom couldn't talk. I told Hazel to tell Mom that I'd be home early the next morning.

Because the drive from Fargo to Westhope took many hours, and I'd be away from home for days, I set about mowing the lawn. The roar of the lawnmower's engine drowned out my guilty crying, which exploded like cloudbursts. After mowing, I went to bed and got up at one o'clock for the dark drive home. I got to Mom's house at sunrise. She was already up, nervously scurrying about. Just after eight o'clock we heard a knock on the door. It was Aunt Ruth, Mom's other sister, the first of many townsfolk to arrive with food and condolences.

When Mom and I were at the funeral home with the minister, she told a story I'd never heard before. She described for the minister how Dad's mother, Dessie, had had to live in a tent behind the house the last summer she was alive so that she wouldn't infect anyone with her tuberculosis. Dessie died in 1920. As Mom continued talking that day, I remember thinking about Grandpa Sam, widowed at age thirty-six with four young children. I also remember thinking that Dad, the youngest, was only a teenager at the height of the Great Depression, and he was in his early twenties when North Dakota's population reached its historical peak, so in some ways he'd witnessed the worst and the best of North Dakota's rural culture during the prime of his life. I remember, too, that Mom wound up her talk with the minister that day by reflecting on Dad's civic-mindedness. She said, "Westhope was his town."

I've since wondered what my paternal great-grand-father considered to be his town—his place. Oblong, Illinois, or Westhope, North Dakota? O. M. spent more than fifty years of his life in Oblong and only fifteen in Westhope, but I'm guessing his choice of burial site answers my question. He and his wife, Dicea, a widower and widow before marrying each other, lay in the Westhope Cemetery.

If I were able to ask O. M. to describe himself, he might say "farmer," but I would argue with him that this choice of description is limiting because it relates only to vocation. When pressed further, he might say instead "father," a definition I would tell him makes more sense to me because he was father to twenty children: nine stepchildren (Dicea's children from her marriage to Dennis Allen); nine children of his own from his marriage to Betsy Ann Allen, a sister to Dennis; and two more children from his marriage to Dicea, one of which was my great-aunt Sylvia, Dad's surrogate mom.

If I attempted to convince O. M. that the philosophy he brought to farming was that of an artist, someone willing to risk all for his craft, I'm willing to bet that he would sadly shake his head and conclude, either silently or out loud, that I've had too much schooling. He might tell me I've spent too much time thinking instead of laboring at tasks that needed doing. Nonetheless, my thinking has led me to conclude that a farmer's optimism permeates the spirit and transcends generations so that family, neighbors, community, and the land itself come to depend on this perennial perseverance, a legacy of responsibility I didn't shoulder.

It's planting season. Dad and I are heading home at dusk, and the springtime air is nearly saturated with the smell of moldy earth. The temperature is brisk, just above freezing. After the winter's long silence, a western meadowlark's trill seems so close that I trick myself momentarily into believing the bird is perched on my shoulder, performing only for me. We chug along in our dilapidated black pickup truck, the cab reeking from the commingled odors of sweat, gasoline, diesel, and grease. Then Dad points to a shelterbelt of trees a half mile away and says, "The old man always said that when you can look off and see leaves on the trees, it's time to quit seeding." About a decade after Grandpa Sam died, Dad finally stopped calling him "the old man."

The act of Grandpa Sam's looking off is a tool farmers can still use, if they choose to do so. It works whether they farm in North Dakota's Bottineau County or in Crawford County, Illinois. It requires only trees, leaves, and the wisdom to understand. Situated near the box elders where Dad parked our swather and other machinery were some untrimmed buckthorn shrubs. The hedge ran within a few feet of the outhouse that Grandpa Sam liked to use during the summer months. Never having experienced air-conditioning, he was fond of shade.

When I asked about those shrubs a couple of years after Grandpa Sam died, when I was seven or eight, Dad told me Grandpa Sam had used a walking plow and our horse Patches to break the ground. Then Dad took me to the small sheep pasture north of our house and showed me the rusting one-bottom plow, which was being swallowed by prairie grasses. He explained how to hook a horse to it, but I've long since forgotten this lesson because the plow seemed antiquated and therefore unnecessary. How foolhardy to worship the complexity of modernity. If I were a lyricist, I would attempt to write an anthem for simplicity and hope, something similar to Keith Secola's "Indian Cars."

Rather than from memory, my images of Grandpa Sam mostly come from snapshots and from watching the choppy, poorly lit eight-millimeter home movies Dad shot. Not so long ago I watched a few minutes of those home movies, which I've transferred to videotape, and for a moment I was confused. I saw Grandpa Sam walking toward me on the TV screen (circa 1958), but what I thought I was seeing was Uncle Chet, circa 1995. Different old men, the same gait. Likewise, a portrait of Grandpa Sam as a younger man hangs in our home and reminds me that I've inherited his ears, not his hair.

Other memories and details occasionally come back to me like unexpected gifts, revealing the unique sense of community that small-town living can forge. For example, I'd forgotten that Mom's sisters, Ruth and Goldie, and almost all of Mom and Dad's friends called Grandpa Sam "Pop." But when I went home once a few years before Mom died, Ruth dropped by for a visit and the conversation turned in such a way that she asked Mom a question, which I've since forgotten, except for its essence, concerning Pop. It's been longer than half a lifetime since the day I stayed with Goldie because Mom and Dad felt their only child was too young to attend Pop's funeral. What went unsaid then was that at this particular funeral my parents and everyone else I knew were likely to be crying. I was playing in Goldie's yard when the hearse carrying Grandpa Sam and the procession of mourners' cars passed by, headed east to a resting place where a shade-throwing shrub grows today.

Dad, still visible in the distance, the lightness of his pith helmet contrasting with the darkness of an olive green work shirt as he steers a tractor with no cab. It's the season of renewal, planting time, and the tractor he drives is moving across a field, pulling a rusty four-bottom plow, an iron-hued packer, and a pony drill with faded green paint. Following behind this mechanized caravan in the cloud of dust it raises are seagulls, some hanging in the air and others swooping to pluck earthworms that the plow's mirrorlike moldboards have uncovered. The faint, rhythmic scream of the seagulls and the drone of the tractor engine conspire to put me to sleep. As I awaken after my nap, my nostrils flare while taking in the moldy smell of the freshly turned earth. Sunlight relaxes muscles in my face, years too young for whiskers.

Despite my disagreements with Dad concerning the work ethic, I am convinced he was a good farmer, although not a good businessman. In April 1974, Dad's best friend, Albert Madsen, died, and his widow, Nell, needed someone to put in the crop. Even though it was an abnormally wet spring, with planting postponed for enough weeks to affect yield, Dad and one other neighbor put in Albert's crop. Dad's help came before he'd planted a bushel of grain on our farm. Even before Albert's funeral, yet another farmer, an agribusinessman, called Albert's landlord and inquired about renting the land Albert would no longer farm. The landlord told Nell about the inquiry, but he rented his land to the inquirer nonetheless. People inquire; money talks.

With respect to farming, Dad was an artisan, taught by his dad and grandfather to love what he did, and so Dad made many of his decisions based on what he thought was best for the land, not what was most profitable. In the name of progress, however, the farming traditions my grandpas practiced came under siege in the 1940s, and many farmers my dad's age were unwitting allies in this assault. At the urging, no doubt, of Dad and Uncle Chet, Grandpa Sam switched completely from horses to mechanized power in 1940 when he bought an International Harvester "W-9" tractor. Dad and Chet took turns driving the machine home from Minot, some sixty-five miles away, and as soon as they got home, they took the W-9 out to the field, hooked it to an implement, and promptly got it mired in mud up to its rear axle.

The fond memories Dad held of that day were evident in the soft chuckles he let slip out, filling gaps among the bits of his recollection about the "I-told-you-so" speech Grandpa Sam leveled at Chet and him. It seems that Grandpa Sam's attitude about farm machinery had been fixed years earlier, when his job on a threshing crew was to operate a steam engine, the iron-wheeled cousin to the railroad locomotives that brought materials and the masses to the Great Plains. Somewhat dinosaur-like in both form and function, steam engines bogged down in mud as if it were tar.

Although the W-9's inauspicious initiation made Grandpa Sam feel vindicated in his belief that horseflesh was superior to horsepower, his moral victory was short lived. Dad and Chet removed the fluid from the tractor's rear tires—rubber tires, the latest technology—and by doing so, they corrected the problem. What they didn't understand at the time was that they had moved onto a slippery slope, one permitting only brief, incremental ascensions before long slides ensued. Dad began relying on still more technology to boost his farm's productivity. First, granular fertilizer and weed-killing chemicals such as 2, 4-D, and, finally, gaseous anhydrous ammonia.

To pay for the added cost of those supplies, dubbed off-farm inputs by the agricultural specialists, Dad had to rely more and more on the local banker. I remember how Dad and his friend Albert joked about the banker, how they could tell by his downward gaze (not a good sign) whether he was inclined to approve their loan request.

More cost, more borrowing, more risk, less independence. Chet grew tired of it all and quit farming the year Grandpa Sam died. Chet and Aunt Evelyn took the cash from the sale of their farm and bought a mom-and-pop motel in Williston, North Dakota, which they sold five years later. Chet spent the remaining years of his working life as an hourly wage earner.

Dad retired before the real proliferation of farm chemicals began, which is when I started farming. I soon understood how my road was diverging. One path seemed to be dead-ending at the status quo: the treadmill of never-ending technological necessities and bankers and bureaucrats. The other path, as I saw it, was leading to organic farming, based on a philosophy that rejects man-made fertilizers and pesticides. Done right, organic farming requires raising livestock and many crops, which work in concert to break pest and disease cycles and enhance soil fertility. Organic farming rewards its faithful with higher prices and society with a healthier environment.

Stay in Illinois and play it safe or journey to North Dakota and risk everything? That was a choice my great-grandfather Hulse faced. One of my choices involved farming with or without chemicals. In responding to my challenge, I heard Uncle Cliff's complaints about the pigeongrass; I saw that while Dad might support my attempts to farm organically, many, if not all, of my peers would scoff, and so I behaved unlike my great-grandfather, unlike my grandfather, and unlike my dad. More like my uncle Chet. I strode toward the unfamiliar by taking up permanent residence in a city, which is to say I walked away from a lifestyle, a heritage, my history.

Mom, wiping dry a heavy pan, her back turned to me as I creep into the kitchen. Me, still wearing my Roy Rogers pajamas, spotting her familiar double boiler sitting on a counter. Even though the sunrise has yet to lift the gloomy veil of a dark winter's night, Mom has made several batches of Christmas candy, the chocolate-laden, caramel-oozing, coconut-filled kinds, lined up on waxed paper like toy soldiers at attention. Mom once used up a ten-pound bag of sugar in a single day.

Before she married Dad, Mom worked for several years on a cook car, which basically was a mobile kitchen that shadowed the nomadic threshing crews during the harvest season. Up before the sun at five o'clock, or earlier, pre-paring breakfasts, dinners, suppers, lunches, homemade bread and buns, fresh-baked pies, doughnuts, cookies— and making artful use of leftovers. Until she died, Mom ground cold roast beef and mixed it with mayonnaise, homemade dill pickles, and onions. A tasty spread. Once she brought sandwiches laid thick with this conglomeration to a senior citizens' potluck, and she commented afterward that two men fondly recognized her offering as being the fare of threshers.

Many of Mom's recollections brimmed with clichés such as "the good ol' days." I've come to believe that those tired phrases symbolize the fatigue and perhaps even the despair of her Great Depression–era youth. In her repetitions, I sense the misery of drudgery playing against the pride of hard work, and the dignity it instills. Mom's photos display other benefits of hard work, too. Fun, for instance, as evidenced by the image of Mom and another unidentified farm girl playing catch with an elongated clump of bread dough alongside the cook car.

As I was growing up, I convinced myself that I would someday be a farmer. The fact that I'd gone away to college, graduated, married a "city girl" raised in a town several times the size of Westhope, and worked as a salesman for two years after college did nothing to alter my belief. And so, when Nicki's dad, an attorney, suggested we buy some of Mom and Dad's farm to avoid inheritance taxes, and when Dad and Mom said they were eager to sell, Nicki and I decided our time had come.

Nicki and I arrived in Westhope during the midst of what most likely was its last housing shortage, and so, we lived with Mom and Dad for many months. Almost immediately, we set about improving the place where I'd been raised and where Mom and Dad had lived for thirty years. Dad hired two schoolteachers to paint our barn a rich, deep red. While the painters painted, Dad and I put up a new barbed wire fence around two sides of our horse pasture, with the plan to finish the job during slack time the following summer. The red-topped steel posts complemented the barn's color. In the fall, I painted the kitchen cabinets in a three-color pattern of green, orange, and yellow, and we installed vinyl flooring and a fuel-oil furnace with enough force to double as a hair dryer. The following spring, Nicki painted the house light blue, and the corral fence in an alternating red and white pattern, with the red matching the barn's tone.

During the winter of 1978–79, Mom and Dad lived in a basement apartment that a retired banker and his wife (turned snowbirds) used as a summer residence. Meanwhile, they built a new house in town, which they moved into in March 1979. Once in town, Mom and Dad drove out to the farm nearly every day. Dad visited and fed his horses; Mom retrieved items from the basement and elsewhere in the house. They didn't knock unless Nicki was home.

My resentment built. When Dad and I were completing the second half of the barbed wire fence in July 1979, I was complaining about the hot, dry weather, and I wanted to stress that I had options. I said, "Maybe I should go to chef school."

"Well, I suppose you can try that, too," Dad said. His tone, to my ear, was saturated with sarcasm and the small-town parochialism Nicki and I believed we had experienced firsthand.

And so I quit farming, untangled myself, and got away, almost as easily as sliding out of a swather reel and running lickety-split to an angry grandfather. Nicki and I sold the farmstead and a few acres adjoining it, left Westhope in the late summer, and headed to Fargo and chef school. I had enrolled thinking that creating food comes close to raising food. During that time, a high school friend of mine whose mother was a local gossip told us the rumor in Westhope was that Nicki and I had kicked Mom and Dad off the farm. His news confirmed for us that leaving small-town life behind had been a good move.

However, in chef school, as I was learning about the five mother sauces and punching a clock in area restaurants, I decided I preferred the role of restaurateur to that of employee. But I also concluded that owning a restaurant is a risky, capital-intensive undertaking, like farming, and a restaurant's success partially depends upon employees, representing an unknown something like the weather. After chef school I struggled with several more sales jobs—struggled because money is not my prime motivator, and selling is hard work for the financially uninspired. Finally, I reenrolled in college, became a writer, and now attempt to harvest subject matter.

When our first basset hound died, Nicki and I decided to bury her in the pasture Grandpa Sam and I had once traversed. Many times during the two seasons we farmed, I drove along Highway 83 north of our farmstead and looked east, only to see a white spot out near the five cottonwoods in our pasture. That spot was Tanya, who scratched at the shed door to be let out around eight o'clock every sunny summer morning, and scratched again to be let in near five o'clock in the evening. During the interim, she nearly always managed to find fresh horse manure to roll in. Many times she appeared on the stoop awaiting her supper with her fur green where it should appear white and with small beads of blood on her nose, evidence that she'd been trying to torment kittens, and again losing the fight. This stoop, the same one from which Grandpa Sam had barked out his orders to me years before.

After Mom died in 2003, Nicki and I cleaned out the home of a Great Depression–era woman who saved things: a stainless steel milk pail, for example, with holes in its rusty bottom, apparently capable of holding only mouse droppings. When Mom and Dad moved into their home in town, they used Grandpa Sam's walking plow as a yard ornament. Eventually, a green ash tree volunteered to grow up in such a way that the tree would have to be sacrificed to move the plow. I asked Uncle Cliff what he thought we should do. He said, "It's a nice tree." We let the plow stay in the shade and become the property of the house's new owner.

In 2004 Westhope celebrated its centennial, and a lot of nostalgic conversations occurred. During one I had with Cliff, he told me that the original Hulse farm contained a chunk of native prairie. I can only imagine how the big bluestem and little bluestem commingled with the switchgrass and the needlegrass and the wheatgrass, the bluestem turning red in the fall and dotting the landscape with contrast.

I also was reminded by these reminiscences that Great-grandpa O. M.'s second wife, Dicea, became confused in her old age. Once, during a summer in the late 1930s, she wandered away from Sylvia's home, where she lived after O. M. had died. The rescue party found Dicea the next morning, about a mile from Sylvia's home, in the pasture where Grandpa Sam and I would eventually take our rides.

Dad told me Dicea had covered her legs with a blanket of sandy soil to keep warm during the night.

I've concluded that Grandpa Sam and I planted the seed that sprouted into my love for the land during those rides in our pasture. While I remain an absentee landlord, I still believe that city life is sustainable only when the countryside is healthy, and I don't see myself ever becoming so far removed from farming to think otherwise. Those five cottonwoods still stand, stubbornly, in our pasture, amid a landscape nearly as depopulated as Jerusalem after its fall. Hoping that the pasture can become a path for me once again, I visit this place several times each year, often alone. I watch our renter's Black Angus cattle amble, as the seconds turn into minutes, becoming nearly an hour. I listen for wind running through grass, a sound that could be the ghostly rustle of Dicea's dress, for the nearby bawling of calves and the miles-away mooing of a former neighbor's Hereford and Red Angus cattle, for the faint cry of hungry seagulls, for the occasional bark of a fox or a farm dog.

In Wendell Berry's novel *Hannah Coulter*, the narrator tells readers that her forty-eight-year-old son Caleb is unaware of emotions and decisions awaiting him as he nears retirement age. She says, "I think he might want to come home then, having been homesick for most of his life." Berry's fiction is my strange truth, but unlike his Caleb, I already know that time and human nature are working against me.

I hold a postindustrial vision of home, and of my homecoming, that is neither nostalgic nor utopian, merely untried. I see a community as accepting of new ideas and different cultures as its members are supportive of people

who grieve. I see a landscape dotted by modern wind tur-
bines providing electricity and independence. Pastures
and rangeland supporting four-stomached animals grazing in patterns mimicking the great bison herds. Farmland
producing not one crop annually, but many, growing in
the same field. Perennials, whose seeds can be separated
at harvest for food and fuel, and whose fiber can be converted into fuel and other products. I see freedom, democracy, and country folk, plenty of them.

Acknowledgments

Even though these essays took more years to live than to write, the writing didn't come without expenses, which in my case are denominated as debts of gratitude.

First, I'd like to thank the University of Minnesota Press, especially Todd Orjala, Laura Westlund, and Andrea Patch, for guidance and patience during the publishing process. My appreciation also goes to Mary Byers, a skillful, tactful copy editor.

Second, Mark Vinz, Alan Davis, and Lin Enger—authors all—invested much time and energy in helping me form early drafts of many of these essays. Their contribution to creative writing vis-à-vis the MFA program at Minnesota State University Moorhead is immense. As for their MSUM colleague photographer Wayne Gudmundson, I value his advice and other assistance.

Third, Ryn Pitts, Karen Kohoutek, Jane Ahlin, Carol Kapaun Ratchenski, and Debra Dawson were members of a writers group that helped me expand, polish, and improve these essays. My friend Barry Brissman was a constant source of encouragement and inspiration.

Finally, my wife, Nicki, deserves highest praise for her flawless support of me and my work.

Dean Hulse is a freelance writer and an activist for issues of land use, renewable energy, and sustainable agriculture. He lives in Fargo, North Dakota.